GEARED

FOR

GROWTH

GEARED
FOR
GROWTH

A PARABLE ABOUT TRANSFORMING
YOUR BUSINESS INTO
A SUCCESS & PROFITS MACHINE

JON TOY

Copyright © 2015 Jon Toy

CONTENTS

Acknowledgments

There are many people I wish to thank for their assistance in bringing this book to completion and helping me launch my platform. I am grateful to all who have encouraged and challenged me through the years. This list is not all-inclusive but represents many who have helped me achieve milestones and goals.

First, thanks be to God, for talents and abilities to be used for His glory.

Thank you to my beautiful wife Crystal for her loving support and friendship, And for being my best friend and the greatest mom in the world to our three lovely children.

Thank you to key accountability partners who always drive me to be the best, and challenge my thinking when I aim too low. Special thanks to Kim Walsh-Phillips for her wisdom in many areas of business growth and her constant drive to be the best. It has helped me see things I was missing.

Thank you to my business coach Mike Capuzzi who challenges me to always improve and try new things that keep the business moving. His support and guidance have given me clarity and strategy when needed.

My mentors through the years who inspired me to be better and keep working hard: My parents, Aaron Hulse, Dr. Rick Lytle, Ed Staub, Charlie McDermott, Mike Capuzzi, Kim Walsh-Phillips, Mike and Kim Gilpin, and the Legacy Board.

Finally, Dan Kennedy for his consistent teachings, challenging the status quo, and strategies that work! His ideas and platform have changed my mindset and ability to succeed.

INTRODUCTION

Owning a small business is tough.

If you are among the many small business owners in this country you can relate. Yet it shouldn't always be tough. Owning a small business should allow you to do what you want to do when you want to do it.

This book is about changing the way you think about your business to make it work for you, not you always working for your business! To do this you must make changes that will happen automatically through proper systems and procedures.

This parable describes everyday situations any business owner can relate to. While it may focus on a few industries, the principles can be applied to any business.

As you read through this story imagine your business taking some of the steps described. How could this work for you? What challenges have you experienced that might be similar to those of the main character?

There are three goals to this book:

1) Create a new way of thinking about your business

2) Establish a structured strategy to implement ideas and improvements

3) Inspire action to transform your business.

It's my belief that you can read this book, take notes, take advantage of the free resources provided at GearedForGrowthBook.com/Bonus, and take action. As a result, your business can be transformed into a Success and Profits Machine.

Through my work with many small business owners—in a variety of different industries not discussed in this book—the strategies from the Machine have been implemented to success.

As you read, decide which of the five gears seems to need the most work in your business. Latch on to one or two of the concepts presented in the parable, and take action.

Action = Profit.

Ideas = Someday?

I want you to reap the most success possible from your business. I hope this book will inspire you to take new actions to keep improving.

You own your business. Take action to make it exactly what you want it to be.

Chapter 1

THE CASH LOSS

The door swung open and Rick Baylor looked up from his seat in the comfortable, almost fancy, waiting area of M&M Garage. This was no ordinary waiting area. The floor was nicely polished and clean, and there were a few separate lounges with nice comfortable couches and chairs. Most garages smelled like gasoline and burnt coffee, but not M&M Garage. Even the flush-mounted flat screen TV was set at a reasonable volume.

Martin, the garage owner, walked over to Rick to explain to him the services needed.

"Mr. Baylor, I want to discuss with you the repairs that wlll be needed on your vehicle. It appears the first and third gears in the transmission have some damage. I don't think it's major. I can probably get in there and fix it up for you today, but it's a fairly labor intensive process. It will be a bit more than what we originally thought. I know once we get in there and make a few of these adjustments your car will run great for you for quite a long time with only slight maintenance needed. Are you okay if we proceed?"

Rick took a deep breath.

He mentally surveyed his balance sheet, knowing he didn't have much extra cash. Yet this was his only vehicle. It wasn't like he could just take the bus to work. So he agreed with Martin and told him to proceed with the repairs.

"I guess it's a cost of life. Good ol' cars... you can't live without 'em and they always seem to suck cash. Thanks, Martin."

Rick Baylor had known Martin for years and used him for all his repairs. Whether it was his own car or his wife's—or now their son's vehicle—Martin always took care of their needs.

They hadn't known each other until several years prior when Rick's car had broken down. He'd had it towed to the nearest garage—M&M—where Martin was particularly friendly and thorough. The garage owner even asked him things early on about him and his family that struck Rick as a little weird.

Martin had sat down with him and went through a series of questions about the vehicle and its history. Then he asked a few personal questions like "What is your address?" and "When is your birthday?" and "When did you purchase your vehicle?"

A few months later, Rick realized why Martin had asked those questions when he received a personalized birthday card and an offer to come in for a brake check-up with a discount coupon. Several months later he received a reminder card for his oil change. And just last month he'd received a "Happy Birthday to Your Car" card in the mail. This time the promotion offered a free oil change and car wash with tire rotation and belt servicing purchase.

Martin knew how to stay in touch and Rick appreciated that. It made him feel like he was part of the M&M Garage family.

But unfortunately for Rick, being a part of this family meant he was going to have to put more money into his car.

At least Rick had the last offer he received from Martin via email handy and would save at least $20 off the final bill.

Chapter 2

EVERY DAY'S A HOLIDAY

Rick walked over to the single-cup brewing machine placed neatly on the counter in one corner of the waiting area and poured himself another cup of coffee. He topped it off with a little cream and sugar and returned to his seat. In preparation for what he'd known might be a lengthy wait, he had brought a few things from work to review.

As he shuffled through the prior week's reports he sighed as he realized it had been yet another month of decreased revenues over the prior month and year-to-date sales were lower than expected.

Rick Baylor owned Maximum Impact Signs and Graphics. He had purchased the company about five years prior from its original owner who never did a whole lot with the business, but seemed to have a nice life and decent cash flow.

Rick was much more ambitious and planned to grow the business to turn it into a large thriving enterprise. He wrote lofty goals, had a great business plan, and was ready to turn this sign and graphic shop into the next small business success story.

Unfortunately for Rick, the last few years had not gone as planned. Sales had plateaued and now were starting to decrease. He was frustrated, tired, and not sure exactly what to do about it.

The sigh he let out piqued the curiosity of another man sitting in the waiting room. The older man calmly and politely asked, "Something in those papers got you feeling a little down?"

Rick looked up and replied, "Well, everyday's a holiday... right?"

The man answered with a smile. "I can appreciate that, but I also sense a bit of sarcasm in that reply, correct?"

"Sure," muttered Rick. *But if I keep telling myself that, surely it will come to pass*, he thought to himself.

"I'm Bill, Bill Burchess. Nice to meet you." The man extended a hand to Rick.

"Rick Baylor," he stated back and made the firm handshake.

"What line of work has you sighing like that, Rick?" Bill inquired.

Rick paused before answering, wondering, *Do I really want to talk about this to a total stranger? What could he possibly know about a sign company? What could he possibly know about even owning a business? Surely he doesn't expect*

me to just open up and pour out my frustrations.
This isn't a psychiatrist's office, it's the waiting
area of a local garage.

"Well, I wouldn't want to bother you with all my
issues, Bill. I wouldn't want to make this any less a
'holiday' to you."

"I doubt you would bother me any. Go ahead and
try, Rick..."

Chapter 3
Unexpected Realization

 Rick looked down at his papers one last time, sighed deeply, and thought, *What do I have to lose?*

"Well for one thing I own a small business, and that comes with its own challenges," Rick stated. "Each day has new problems and fires that always require my attention. I never seem to know what might come at me when I get in the office. Sometimes even appointments like this—that cost me money—can be an escape. But if you've never been a business owner it probably doesn't make much sense to you."

The older man grinned and let out a small chuckle. "Rick, I think I understand your world all too well. You see I too owned a small business."

Somewhat shocked, Rick immediately regretted his prior words.

He had pre-judged the old man and hadn't even thought about asking him what he did, or where he lived... or really *anything* at all. He had been so consumed with his own problems he just assumed it was another old man hanging out at the garage.

Rick stumbled over his words as he expressed, "I'm sorry, Bill. That was a rather frustrated comment. I didn't mean to..."

Bill cut him off. "Son, you can't offend me. I've been through it all. Owning a business teaches you a lot about people, problems, and especially how to get better.

"So tell me a bit more about some of the struggles you are facing. I might not be an expert, but I did have great success before I sold my business and retired just a few years ago."

Rick decided he might as well share a few of his current struggles to see what kind of perspective the old man might have for him.

He was open to new ideas and wisdom.. Cash flow was tight, accounts receivable was creeping higher and higher, sales were down, and he felt like his team at the shop never wanted to do more or go the extra mile.

It can't be too much worse, he thought. *Why not see if Bill Burchess can offer some insight?*

"Well, Bill..."

Rick's cell phone started ringing and buzzing at just that moment. Distracted he asked, "I'm sorry, can you just excuse me for one second? It's the shop."

Chapter 4

TROUBLE AT THE SHOP

 Rick walked out the door into the sunlight and answered his phone.

"Hello, this is Rick." He knew it was the shop, but that was his customary greeting, just in case it was someone else or the Caller ID on his cell phone wasn't right for some reason.

Secretly he always hoped it wasn't right and they weren't calling to tell him about some issue that needed his help.

"Rick," the voice on the other end stammered along. "One of the printers just broke down and I can't figure it out, and the phones keep ringing today so Julie is all tied up. I can't answer the phone if I possibly want to get anything done today. When are you going to be back?"

Brian was Rick's primary printer operator and helped out in sign production back at the shop. He had been with Rick for about three years. A good worker, Brian was always on time and would stay late as needed, but Rick wished he would take some initiative once in a while instead of always relying on him for answers.

"Brian, calm down just a minute. Why are you calling me? You know I can't fix the printer. What have you done to try and get this resolved?"

Brian fumbled for words and said, "Well, I restarted the printer and the computer and then I called you. That didn't seem to work."

"Okay, well what else do you think you could try until I get back?" Rick asked.

"I don't know. That's why I'm calling you. Julie keeps bugging me to answer the phones when she is with someone. I can't do that right now. There's just too much going on. Are you going to be back soon?"

Frustrated, Rick continued, "Brian, did you try calling tech support at the vendor? Or did you reach out to our salesman to find out who else has this printer that you could contact? Did you call the manufacturer and see what tech support options they might have?"

"No, where would I even find all those phone numbers?"

"Brian, you know where to find all this information. It's in the 'playbook.' Remember when I showed you where to find all the important documents? It's on the shared drive under the folder 'playbook,' then 'printer information.' All the numbers are in one document and the printer manual is in another. It should have all you need to reach out and get answers. Do that, then go help in production and answer the phones with Julie until someone can help you. Can you do that?"

"Yes, Rick. That makes sense. I do remember you showing me one time where that was, but we didn't spend a lot of time discussing it. I'll check it out and see if I can find those numbers. Thanks."

Rick hung up the phone, shaking his head. He knew he had shown Brian where to find all those documents. After all, he had spent a tremendous amount of time creating the playbook so it would help everyone know right where to look for important documents.

In hindsight, he realized he probably didn't do a good job of training the team on what the playbook was, what was in it, or how they should all be using it.

Rick's background was in manufacturing. He had previously been the manager of a large plant in the area. He had strong experience in operations—but sales and market were where he struggled.

One of his first duties as owner was to create the company playbook. He knew the biggest differences between big businesses and small businesses was operating systems and procedures.

Rick had invested a lot of time gathering all the steps to do each position in the company, all the important forms and documents, and even creating detailed checklists to help everyone know exactly what to do each day.

It was supposed to eliminate the need for constant questions and interruptions.

Yet in thinking back to his roll-out of the playbook to his team, he didn't do a good job of training them or explaining how and why to use it. Rick had scheduled a training, but it was interrupted by customer needs and they never re-visited the playbook as a group.

He jotted down a note to make sure he scheduled some time to go over everything that was in that playbook with his team. Rick wanted to be sure they all understood the value of it and what was in it.

This interruption had been exactly the type of call the playbook was supposed to eliminate.

Rick shook his head and could only smile and laugh at himself as he wondered how he got into this mess.

He walked back into the waiting area, ready to engage in conversation with someone he hoped could shed some light on what he could be doing better.

Rick was in for quite a surprise at just how much Bill could help him with the challenges of running a small business.

Rick's Notebook:

	Date · No.

set team training time
for playbook.
be sure to review procedures
And update as needed

**To download resources and tools to help you grow,
visit: www.GearedForGrowthBook.com/Bonus**

Chapter 5

CHOCOLATE EXPERIENCE & A MACHINE

 Rick walked back into the waiting room, head hung low, shaking side to side.

Bill asked politely, "Everything okay back at the farm?"

Bill had a professional manner about him when speaking yet Rick could tell he was hiding a grin. He obviously knew Rick needed assistance.

"I guess so. It's the same old thing all the time. Someone relies on me to do something they should know how to do, and I get sucked into the unproductive work of putting out fires instead of revenue-producing activity," Rick stated.

Bill grinned widely. "Rick, let's go next door to the diner. I know the owner. They have a great special everyday and I think it's happy hour for the sodas. I'll treat and we can discuss some things that might be of assistance to you."

Rick agreed. They put on their coats and walked out the door, headed across the street to the All Star Diner.

At the restaurant's entrance they were immediately greeted by a friendly face. "Welcome to the All Star Diner. My name is Wendy and I'd be happy to help you. Two for dining? Or is there something else I can assist with?"

Rick had been in the restaurant once, but it had been several years before. He certainly didn't remember this type of friendly service and greeting... especially for a local diner.

Bill interjected with a pleasant, "Hi, Wendy. I'm Bill Burchess and here is my All Star Card." Bill handed her a small plastic card that had a nice design with his name imprinted.

Wendy smiled and said, "Of course, Mr. Burchess. I didn't recognize you. Are you losing weight? Right this way to our VIP area. Did you want a Coke today, or Sweet Tea?"

Bill replied, "How about a Coke? I could use some sugar this afternoon. Rick, what would you like to drink?"

"I'll take a Coke too, thanks," Rick muttered, still amazed at what was happening in this little diner.

Wendy smiled at Rick and asked if it was his first time in the restaurant.

"Well, no. But I sure feel like it. It's been a long time and it definitely wasn't this nice a few years ago," Rick answered.

Wendy smiled again and said, "We take great pride in making sure our guests feel this is just like home. We want you to return and bring your friends and family. If you don't mind, I'll leave this guide for you to review."

Wendy gently placed a nicely printed small packet on the table with an imprinted pen with the restaurant logo next to Rick. "We would love to have you join our All Star VIP program just like Mr. Burchess. There is no charge and as you can see, we make sure it's an All Star experience for you each time."

"Thank you. I think I will," Rick replied.

Wendy seated them and stated that their All Star Server Jennifer would be with them shortly.

They sat down in a nice booth with very clean seats and tabletop. It was absent the usual diner apparel of metal holder with sloppily tossed salt and pepper shakers and dirty ketchup

> *Not new owners, just a new mindset.*

containers. The table was completely empty and clean. Rick was impressed.

"Wow, this diner has really changed since the last time I was in. I wonder what made the difference? New owners maybe?"

Bill chuckled and said, "No, not new owners. Just a new mindset. I know Tony the owner quite well. He and I have worked together to make some changes here over the past few years. And he and his customers are VERY pleased. In fact they have more than tripled their business in the last three years. He is opening two more diners in town and I expect both will be filled to capacity much like this one quickly."

Wow, tripled the business? Rick's mind raced, imagining his own numbers times three. What would his little sign shop do if they could triple their business? How many employees would he have, what type of technololgy would he need, how would they ever keep up?

Bill coughed politely. Rick realized he'd drifted far away from their conversation.

Bill had a good strong smile that seemed to comfort Rick. It was as if Bill could read his mind and wanted to assure him everything would be okay.

The waitress Jennifer brought them each their drinks and thanked them for coming to the All Star Diner and introduced herself. She asked their permission to share the specials of the day, to which they obliged. She described in savory detail two special lunch options available only for that day. Both sounded so great Rick's stomach started making noises. He realized he hadn't eaten lunch. *A common occurrence*, he thought. His busy days at the sign company, combined with his many responsibilities, often made him forget to eat.

After Jennifer described the two specials she asked a question that truly caught Rick off guard.

"Now our best special of the day is our Decadent Chocolate Experience dessert."

The name alone made Rick's mouth water. She went on to describe this amazing chocolate dessert with many extras added in to make it a one of a kind experience. The final statement was what truly blew Rick's mind...

"Now in order to experience this one of a kind dessert, you have to place your order before your meal. This may sound quite unusual, however we have to be sure we prepare this experience just right and if we rush to complete it at the end, it just won't give you the decadent experience our owner Tony wants you to receive. Would you gentlemen be interested in enjoying this unique experience each by yourself? Or sharing it together?"

Rick's jaw dropped. He couldn't believe it. Not only was it a great sales pitch, he had *never* had anyone at a restaurant ask him for his dessert order *before* ordering his meal—and practically right after sitting down. It was the most masterfully crafted offer he had ever experienced. And this was just a diner, not a five-star steakhouse.

"Ummm, I'm not sure I know what to say, Jennifer. That sounds amazing," was all Rick could get out.

"It is truly amazing and you would be joining over a hundred other customers who chose the experience just this month already. So two? Or just sharing one?" Jennifer continued.

Bill chimed in, "Jennifer, I think we will share one. And when you get a chance, tell Tony that Bill Burchess is here and would like to say hi."

"Thank you, gentlemen. I'll give you a chance to review the menu and consider your lunch options while I begin the Decadent Chocolate Experience for you."

She walked away briskly, stopping briefly to converse with her other customers, smiling and laughing with each table she visited.

"Bill, this place is amazing. What on earth did you teach Tony, and how did he make it happen?" Rick asked.

"Rick, this is exactly what I want to teach you today. I see you have your notebook, so be ready to take notes and let's see if we can't help you make a few tweaks to your business.

"The first thing I want you to know is that your business is a MACHINE. It runs like a machine, it breaks down like a machine and it needs tweaking and maintenance like a machine. It's just that this machine produces money. You put one dollar in and you get more than one dollar out. That's the goal," Bill stated confidently.

Rick nodded his head and opened up his notebook, pen already moving.

> *Your business is a MACHINE. It runs like a machine, it breaks down like a machine and it needs tweaking and maintenance like a machine. It's just that this machine produces money.*

Bill started again, "You see, Rick, if you can understand the machine and make the right adjustments, it will work all day long for you—instead of *you* working all day for *it*. In fact..."

"BILL!" a loud voice boomed from a few feet behind them. "How in the world are you? So good to see you, and you even brought a friend!"

It was the owner of All Star Diner, Tony Miller.

Rick's Notebook:

Date · No.

- my business is a MACHINE

- I need to perform
  maintenance and tweak the
  machine regularly

- $1 In = >$1

Chapter 6

IDEAS INTO ACTION

Tony Miller was a large man, dressed nicely and looked to be in his mid fifties. He had a big comforting smile and seemed like the kind of guy you would want to be friends with. He slapped Bill on the back and as Bill rose to say hello, Tony wrapped his arms around him in a big bear hug.

"Bill, it's always a pleasure to have you here. So what brings you in today?"

"I just met Rick next door and we were about to discuss some ways he might be able to improve his business. What better place to show and tell than All Star Diner? Tony, you really have done an amazing thing here," Bill said with a certain proud father look.

"Well, it's all thanks to you, Bill. Seriously, Rick, we would never have made the changes we made without him. I was a struggling diner owner with bad employees, bad customers, and nothing unique about us-versus-everyone-else in town. I hired Bill five years ago and was in real need of help. He provided the ideas and the strategy. I provided the hard work and implementation. You know, Rick, I don't know you, but as a business owner if you focus all your energy on getting important projects done—and not just doing the work—you can transform your business fast." Tony was clearly excited and bragged happily of his success.

Bill chimed in, "Tony, you're a heck of a worker. You had the drive and the attitude and most importantly the vision to be great. I just provided some clarity."

They visited for a few minutes as Rick sat back and took in the whole experience. What had he just gotten himself into? Clearly Bill was influential, successful, and just a nice guy. He was already sharing with Rick... and Rick hadn't paid him a dime.

Rick knew he needed to take good notes, see what he could learn from this diner, from Bill, and from their conversation.

Rick had always been a motivated guy. He went to seminars and trade shows for the sign industry. He read books on business when he could, and generally wanted to make his sign company the best business it could possibly be. Unfortunately he felt much more like the Tony Miller described from five years ago than the Tony Miller he saw happily talking to Bill and enjoying a completely different lifestyle and business.

What was the difference? What in the world had Bill taught him? Rick had to learn more.

Chapter 7

CONVERSATION

Bill and Tony wrapped up their conversation and Tony smiled at Rick. "Stick with this guy, he can show you the ropes. In fact, if I were you, I'd hire him today and figure it all out tomorrow! I hope you'll come back to All Star Diner and bring your family. In fact here is a return reward card—you can have a free entrée with the purchase of another on your next visit. Hope to see you soon!"

Tony whisked off and back to his daily activities. Bill commented that unlike most restaurant owners, Tony spends most of his day planning customer acquisition strategies and marketing. He hires good people and holds them accountable to do the rest so he can focus on growing the daily number of happy full-stomach customers that will come back time and time again.

Rick was still amazed by not only the conversation but what he was experiencing at All Star Diner. He sat back in his seat and took a deep, noticeably audible breath. All he could think was, "*Wow.*"

Bill smiled his normal, calm smooth smile and said to Rick, "Are you ready to get started discussing this Machine process I mentioned to you?

"You see, Rick, this business... like your business and like my business... has certain core elements—I call them gears—that keep your machine running and producing a profit. Each gear is independent but they work together as a whole to make the machine run fast, efficiently, and profitably.

"Let's talk about the first gear, it's truly the foundation of every business and it's what most businesses put little or no resources, training or incentives into. Any guesses on what one of the most important parts of every business is?" Bill inquired.

> *Your business has core elements—gears—that keep your machine running and producing a profit. Each gear is independent but they work together to make the whole machine run fast, efficiently and profitably.*

"Customer service?" Rick answered.

"Well, you're close, Rick, but businesses spend thousands of dollars on customer service every year. It's very important to have good customer service, but what really drives customer service?

How does customer service even get the chance to interact? Getting there is the foundation.

"The first gear is called CONVERSATION."

Rick jotted that down in his notebook. He had been scribbling notes all along, but now it was really getting good.

"You see, Rick, the conversation is always starting. The conversation with your prospects for your business is always starting. It starts on the phone—which by the way is the answer to my previous question about the most important and underemphasized part of most businesses. It starts on the website. It starts when you meet someone like Tony Miller who might become a customer. It starts when your employees go out on the weekends. The conversation—first gear—is always happening and it always starts with prospects.

"Now I haven't had the chance to talk much about my business, Rick, but I was the owner of TB's Hardware. Are you familiar with the company?" Bill asked.

"Well of course, Bill. I mean they seem to be the only hardware store in this part of the country that can stay open and compete with the two big dogs of the industry. Even the smaller hardware chains are falling by the wayside quicker and quicker. Wow, TB's is a pretty big business, isn't it?" Rick asked.

"Yes, at our peak we had over 500 employees. And with six locations across the region, our average sales per employee are the highest in our industry. I'd say we did alright. It was a mighty journey and I loved every minute. But, Rick, it took hard work and a lot of thinking—thinking *differently* than every other hardware store out there. I had to change the mindset of my team to make it work, and to make it so profitable.

"So let me share with you first the most important part of the Conversation and of the first gear—the phones."

Rick's Notebook:

Date

- My machine has gears
  Independent but work
  Together

- FIRST GEAR: CONVERSATION

- Conversation is always
  starting

- Phones are the most
  important

To download resources and tools to help you
grow, visit:
www.GearedForGrowthBook.com/Bonus

Chapter 8

THE LIFELINE OF BUSINESS

 "What is your expectation of your team when they answer the phone, Rick?" Bill quizzed him.

"Well, I guess to be friendly and knowledgeable and help the person get what they wanted from calling us. Give them great customer service—although based on your prior comment, I'm guessing I might be missing a few things." Rick smiled but inside he knew he and his team were missing the boat on this area.

"You are about one-sixth right. So not all is lost. Rick, almost every business has friendly people that care about their work answering the phones. That's pretty much par for the course. If someone isn't friendly, then no one will call back. So that's the easy part.

"The hard part is having a system for answering phones that drives business and gets results. Now you might have sales people that think they are doing a good job or that think they know how to answer a phone. And they probably do okay, but I can almost guarantee if you don't have a system—and aren't training and rewarding on it—those folks are doing things wrong and costing you as the business owner thousands of dollars a day, or a month, or worse... even an hour.

"We monetized it in our hardware business before we changed the way we answered the phones and determined it had been costing us over $5,000 an hour in business. That's $75,000 a day, per store. Do the math and that's a lot of money slipping right through the cracks. So your number might not be that bad, but it's a multiplier number that gets worse day by day if not corrected.

"So why does this happen? Simple, lack of clarity and expectations on what the purpose of a phone call is. So we constructed a system and then trained it, monitored it daily, then rewarded it."

Rick looked puzzled, "I'm confused. What could you possibly have changed that made up $5,000 an hour? That seems ridiculous just because of the way a phone call was handled."

"Indeed it was. How do you think I felt when I learned that number? Crazy! But we had not done anything about it. It's all about having a system. So we put in place our 5-Star Phone Training."

"Every call requires 5 Stars –

1. Have a happy and friendly greeting—state your name clearly and the company name clearly and ask how you can help make their day better

2. Make sure you get their name and use it in the conversation
3. Assess their need and try to drive them to the store—we can't make any money if they don't buy from us—you have the ability to control the sale
4. Capture their information and get them to join our TB's Team VIP program
5. Invite them to come in and try to book an appointment to meet with a TB's Hardware Team Personal Consultant

"So that was how we took a desire to better monetize the phones and made it into a set system with metrics.

"After that point we could track the number of calls, the number of appointments booked, and the number of TB's Team VIP sign-ups. Just by tracking those three numbers we were able to go back and determine that prior to implementing the 5-Star system it had been costing us over $5,000 an hour. It was a HUGE revelation for our company.

"This transition didn't happen overnight. It took work and training and coaching, even some firing and re-hiring. It was a process, but it generated an additional $75,000 a day for our stores. We reinvested lots of that additional revenue into driving more traffic to the phones—and in turn bringing that traffic into our stores—and improving our phone process to the point where we had to create an entire phone room just for answering calls and making sure we completed our 5 STARS."

Rick was taking notes furiously, but looked concerned over how this all developed. "So how did you start? Surely there were a lot of other things that had to be happening at the same time to get that $5,000 an hour number, right?"

"Yes, of course," Bill replied.

The waitress brought their food and refilled their drinks... and re-described the decadent

> **The phone is the MOST IMPORTANT part of the conversation gear.**
>
> To get bonus resources and phone answering tips to help you go to:
> GearedForGrowthBook.com/Bonus

dessert that was in process for them. It sounded even better now.

"Let's eat and I'll fill you in on the other CONVERSATION processes we put in place. But remember, the phone is the *most important* part of the conversation gear. It's the foundation for new customer intake and relationship starting. Now dig in."

Rick's Notebook:

To get a copy of a real phone intake form visit:
GearedForGrowthBook.com/Bonus

Chapter 9

Money Goggles

Rick had ordered a hamburger and fries—standard diner food by every measure—however somehow he thought this was more than just an average diner hamburger. He couldn't quite put his finger on what was different but he thought something was much better. He continued eating and posed the question to Bill, "So I understand the phones, and I can see how that would help drive more traffic, but what else had to change? Just changing the way you answer phones couldn't possibly have driven $75,000 a day, could it?"

Bill smiled again as he wiped his mouth from his last delicious bite. Bill had ordered a chicken Caesar salad and it was presented beautifully. It looked like it had been prepared at a fancy steakhouse, not the typical diner with lettuce and chicken and dressing slapped in a bowl.

Bill began, "Well, Rick, you are right in some regards, although I want to emphasize just how important your phones are. If you hear nothing else from me in this conversation, go back and start training your team, monitoring them, and incentivizing how they do with the phones. It's the

41

number one money-leak in small businesses today. Many just aren't doing it well. Friendly? Yes. But making money? No."

He continued, "So what else did we do? We changed quite a lot, but obviously started with the phones. Then we had to make sure our in-store experience matched what we knew our phone service was now providing. I created something called the 'new customer experience' program. I realized that every time a new customer walked through our doors we had one shot at making it the best experience they ever had. One small mistake or frustration, and that customer could be lost forever.

I didn't want to lose anyone, and my team knew that new customers had become a major focus for us.

> *Every time a new customer walked through our doors, we had one shot at making it the best experience.*
>
> For more resources on improving your experience go to:
> GearedForGrowth.com/Bonus

"Everyone had to put on 'new customer goggles' every time they came to work."

Rick laughed, "That sounds like prepping for a swim meet or heading down the ski slopes."

Bill nodded. "That's exactly what it was like, and that is what I taught my team. You see, when you put on your goggles they protect you and let you see more clearly. If we wanted the best customer experience, we needed to protect the new customer and see clearly. So everyday everyone had to put on their 'new customer goggles' and look at our business as if they were the new customer. I quizzed the team regularly by simply asking them, 'If you were a first time customer today, what could have been done better to make this the best experience?'

"My team always knew to be on the lookout for ideas and ways to make it a better experience for the customer. I found that involving the team in the process made it way easier on me. They provided the ideas, and I followed up with the actions to make it happen. Then we watched as so many new customers commented on how wonderful the service was, and how they would drive out of their way to come to our store instead of the competitor's. So don't underestimate the power of putting yourself in a new customer's shoes each time you walk into your business.

"What do they see? What do they hear? Are they greeted well? Does the store look professional and welcoming? How does it smell, and on and on and on. Always keep asking yourself how to make it better."

Rick knew as he envisioned himself walking into his sign shop that he certainly had some work that could be done in this regard. It wasn't horrible, but it certainly didn't scream 'professional' or 'big business ready and willing to serve you' as you walked through the doors. He made a note to work on making better first impressions.

"Wow, Bill. It seems so simple, yet I know we are missing the boat on these two things. And the worst part is, that's just your first gear!" Rick chuckled audibly knowing that if he wanted to transform his business some of these actions would need to happen fast.

Rick was about to ask another question when a tall professional looking man in a nice suit approached their table.

"Bill, so good to see you," the man commented. He had a soft comforting tone, like a good bedside manner, and a perfect smile that put Rick at ease. The man just looked like the type of person he would want to have a conversation with.

He reached out to shake Bill's hand. Instead, Bill rose to shake his hand firmly while embracing him and smiling.

"So good to see you, Doc," Bill said. He turned to the woman who accompanied the well-dressed man and asked, "And how is Mrs. Rose today?"

She was dressed in scrubs, which reinforced Rick's opinion that the man must be some sort of medical professional. "Oh, you're always so sweet, Mr. Bill. I'm doing wonderful. I see you are back at All Star Diner again."

"Well, of course. Tony makes an offer I can't refuse—great food and wonderful service! Plus he's a terrific client and I love seeing what he's doing each time I come in." Bill glanced back at Rick to make sure he was listening before asking them, "You two back for your weekly state-of-the-office manager meeting?" Bill questioned.

The man nodded his head and smiled again. "We won't interrupt your meeting any longer. Just wanted to say hello. I'll talk to you next week. Have a wonderful day."

"You do the same, and make it a productive meeting," Bill said as he sat back down with Rick.

"We always do," the man replied confidently.

Rick was eager to learn more about who the man was. What did Bill do for him, and why were they meeting weekly in a diner?

Bill could tell Rick had questions. "Take another bite and I'll fill you in on Dr. Jim."

Rick's Notebook:

Date · No.

- New Customer Goggles

What do I see when I come in??

What is my experience Like?

Is it impressive?

Does it wow??

Chapter 10

START OUT RIGHT

"That's Dr. Jim Miller. He's a local dentist. I met him years ago at a local Chamber of Commerce event. He was just starting his practice and was overwhelmed by what to do and how to grow.

"We started meeting every so often to discuss how he could make his business different than every other dentist in town. There are so many of them in this region, and of course in this town. He was unsure how he could be different.

> *He created an environment where every new patient feels so welcomed and so at ease about coming there, they can't help but return, refer, and review him.*
>
> For more ideas on how to create a return, refer and review environment go to:
> GearedForGrowth.com/Bonus

"So we worked on a plan to start with the phones—as we already discussed. Then we worked through his new patient experience, and now he's the most successful dentist in town. He created an environment where every new patient feels so welcomed and so at ease about coming there, they can't help but return, refer, and review him. His practice keeps growing double digits every year. He's to the point where he doesn't even see patients much anymore, but rather works on his business so he can help more and more people have the best experience possible at his practice."

"Wow, that sounds a lot better than my dentist. I still dread going and sure don't feel anything special other than a few pokes in the gum," Rick stated while smiling and shoveling another bite of his great burger into his mouth.

Chapter 11

CHOREOGRAPHED SALES

 "So how do you work with him? And what was he talking about when he said you would talk next week?" Rick asked.

"Well, I love helping others and I love teaching. So as I see people with a desire to grow and the ability and willingness to take action, I help them. Jim was one of those people I met years ago and eventually it transformed into a coaching opportunity for me because he wanted more than I was able to give in our occasional breakfast meetings.

"I've had a coaching business for the last five years. I help entrepreneurs just like you figure out where their leaks are and implement the five gears we're discussing right now. It's a formal program that not only allows me to coach one-on-one but also in group settings both online and in-person. I also send out an informative newsletter once a month. Everyone gets a recording, so they can benefit whether or not they were able to attend."

"That sounds like what I need, Bill. We're only on the first gear and I'm impressed. How do I sign up?" Rick asked.

"Slow down, Rick. I'm not charging you for this. We need to be sure you understand how you can change your business before I go and start taking your hard- earned dollars.

"Let's go back to the first gear and look at Jim and Tony whom you met today."

"Both of them have dedicated staff trained heavily on answering the phones. Both of them 'mystery shop' their phones regularly and reward those employees who excel at it, doing what they are trained to do. As a result, those incoming phone calls drive more prospects and customers into their businesses and they see results. You can't get more opposite than a diner and a dentist, yet they use the same 5-Star system we crafted at our hardware stores to drive results from incoming calls.

"Next, they both work very hard on that first experience. Think of when you entered the diner today. What was different?"

Rick sat up a little straighter and said, "Everything! Once you gave them your VIP card, the hostess knew you—or at least acted like she knew you—and complimented you. She asked if you wanted your usual drink and escorted us to a VIP area. Then she asked me if it was my first time and tried to get me to sign up for the VIP program." Rick was amazed how it had made an impression on him.

"Exactly, and do you think that was by chance? No, Tony choreographs the entire process. He trains his hostesses and makes sure they do exactly what he wants done. He tracks everything he can track. It's a designed experience, and he is always tweaking it, right down to that 'Decadent something or other' we are going to be enjoying here shortly. So eat up," Bill smiled.

"And Dr. Jim is the same way. He has trained those answering his phones, and uses an answering service when the office is closed or they are away. He also trained the answering service how he wants them to answer the phones as well. Then when a new patient comes to the practice, they have all types of ways to wow them. Folks receive a gift bag and they are called by name. Rather than having them go to a window and get a clipboard, they are escorted to an office where a personal treatment consultant assists them, and they receive a bottle of water whether they ask for it or not.

> *Remember, Inspect What You Expect!*

"It's all about creating an experience that no one expects, and then leveraging that experience to get the customer to spend more, tell more people, and return. That's the foundation of the first gear. The conversation is always happening.

"Of course there's more, but we can't spend all day on the first gear or you wouldn't ever get back to your business—and you might not get back to your family either," Bill chuckled and took another bite.

51

"Okay, you win. I see how this first gear is so important. I'll be sure to work on that right away when I get back to the office. I know we have room for improvement and those are pretty inexpensive things to fix. More importantly, they're pretty easy!"

"Glad you think so. I'm sure you'll see the results you want. Remember, *inspect* what you *expect*. If you aren't inspecting how the phones are handled, you can't expect them to be done right. Change that one little thing, and you could see double-digit growth rather quickly.

"So should we talk about the second gear before our pre-ordered, and definitely scripted and thought-out—from a sales standpoint—Decadent Chocolate calorie fest arrives?"

Chapter 12

CONVERSION & THE LAW OF THREE

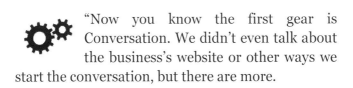"Now you know the first gear is Conversation. We didn't even talk about the business's website or other ways we start the conversation, but there are more.

"But for now let's move on to the second gear, Conversion."

"Let me start by telling you the foundation of these five gears is based on a fact of business known as the

LAW OF THREE

"There are only three ways to grow your business. If you are always working on those three things, you can always be growing your business.

"So here is the Law of Three:

1. Get more new customers
2. Get them to pay more, or increase the transaction value of each customer
3. Get your customers to return more frequently

That's it, the only three ways to grow your business. Now there are a million ways to improve those three things, but if you focus on improving just these three areas—and monitoring them—your business will grow."

"Wow, that seems so simple. I never thought about it that way. It makes perfect sense, yet for some reason all I ever focused on was getting more new customers." Rick looked perplexed.

"Well, Rick, you are not alone. Most small business owners wake up thinking about growth. They ask themselves, 'How do I sell more stuff?' Instead they should be thinking not only about how to sell more stuff, but how to sell more stuff at a higher cost and make more sales to existing customers.

> **You shouldn't isolate just one growth technique. If you only focus on new growth, you have to always be thinking about volume of customers rather than value of customers.**
>
> For ideas on how to improve your Law of Three visit:
> GearedForGrowth.com/Bonus

"You shouldn't isolate just one growth technique. If you only focus on new growth, you have to always be thinking about *volume* of customers rather than *value* of customers.

"The *value* of a single customer can typically be grown as much as five to ten times the original value just by changing the way you think about growth as a business owner.

"Now, you still have to create a regular flow of new leads into your business, but when you shift your mindset to think about all three methods of growth, each new customer will cycle through the three ways and allow you to take an ordinary transaction and turn it into a powerful customer relationship— which is worth so much more in the long run.

"Make sense, Rick?"

"Yes, it does, but I know we don't do a good job of that. And I have no way of knowing even how to start. I mean... if I raise my prices, I know I'll lose customers," Rick explained.

"You may be right, but Conversion is not all about just raising prices. I can tell you most business owners are way too timid about raising prices. They are always afraid of losing business, a client here or there. But by not increasing prices as their own costs rise, instead they wind up losing their whole business.

"Rick, the reality is, you probably aren't charging enough, regardless of what your competitors charge. Obviously you have to be fair and competitive, but there's no reason if you offer a good service and great product you can't charge more than your competitors... and sometimes *much more*.

"Don't you think that hamburger you just ate is going to cost you more than it would at the other diner down the street? It will cost more than even the chain restaurants. Why? Because there is an experience, a quality of product and certainly a level of service that justify its cost. The cost difference is not so much it makes you gasp and not return. After all it's not like they are going to charge you $20 for that burger. If they did you might not return. But by charging just 10-15% more, you won't have a real issue. And they'll earn more money per customer transaction.

"I would definitely urge you to look at your pricing and increase it right away at some level. Even 2-3% won't make a customer really question it, but it will help cover your creeping costs of materials, right?" Bill asked.

"Yes, it would! I haven't raised prices in years. You're exactly right. I know we are in line with our competitors, and we might even be a bit cheaper in some instances. But how does pricing tie in to Conversion? When I hear that word I only think of prospects becoming new customers. If I have higher pricing, it seems like that would take away from someone wanting to become a customer."

"Good observation, Rick. Let's discuss that. Conversion is when a prospect finally agrees to do business with you. So obviously it involves pricing. If the second way to grow your business is to increase what they pay you, then you have to have a solid plan on how to increase the per-transaction value—not only of new customers, but of all customers.

"Pricing is a big part of this. By marginally increasing your prices, your business can grow instantly.

"But there is more you can do to improve the average transaction value of your customers. Just one of the ideas I teach my clients includes offering some type of VIP or Premium service. Did you know that anywhere from 5-20% of all customers will accept the offer just because of their buying habits?

"Perhaps with you, VIP service means they get faster turnaround on projects, or higher priority in repair and maintenance work on signs, or even credits toward their next purchase. I don't know the specifics of your business, but there is an opportunity to add a premium and you are not doing it.

"When you add a premium, you can instantly increase your average transaction value, and thus grow your business.

"Another easy way is to bundle services and products. Let's just say a banner is a very profitable product for you. When someone is ordering one, you could offer a second one for a certain percent discount at the time of purchase. The customer gets a good deal and feels great about it. You maintain good margins on your product, and just because you asked or offered the package, your business instantly earns more.

"Does that make sense, Rick?" Bill quizzed.

"Yes, it does. We certainly have not done any upselling or product packaging. And I never even considered offering a premium product or service. Wow, my brain is on overload! I'm not sure I can handle all five of your gears, Bill," Rick laughed. His head was churning with new ideas and he desperately wished he had been recording this conversation.

Bill laughed in response. "Let's just enjoy our chocolate! Here it comes now."

Rick's Notebook:

Date · No.

- Growth - -the Law of **3**

1 Get more customers!

2 Raise prices/Get more
per transaction

3 Get them to buy more
Frequently

$

Chapter 13

CONVERSION IN ACTION

Rick heard somewhat of a commotion approaching from behind him. As he turned he saw what appeared to be sparklers on top of what could only be their Chocolate Decadent dessert.

Jennifer wheeled it over, sparklers blazing. This dessert was all chocolate and looked amazing. It appeared to be a chocolate cake of some type covered with a special chocolate sauce. It was surrounded by chocolate chips and flakes—not thrown on there randomly, but delicately and precisely placed around the cake. The sparklers shimmered and light seemed to come directly out of the top of the cake. Even better, there was a light peanut butter sauce and peanut butter cups placed strategically against the cake. This was truly decadent.

"Wow!" was all Rick could say about this special treat. He grabbed his fork, ready to devour.

"Well, we certainly will exceed our calorie intake today, Rick... but it's going to be fun!" Bill smiled as he also picked up his fork, ready to dive into the dessert.

"So, Rick, how do you think this special dessert plays into Tony's strategy for increasing customer transaction value and helping his Conversion gear?" Bill inquired between bites.

"Well, it's amazing to me that Jennifer was able to get us to commit to this BEFORE we ordered our meal. I have never heard or seen that before. That's one way to secure dessert order revenue that most restaurants miss out on. I mean typically I'm full after the meal and wouldn't dream of ordering dessert. But if you ask me when I'm hungry, I'm much more likely to commit."

"Exactly," Bill commented.

"And it's certainly not a cheap dessert," Rick continued. "I mean this is no ordinary sundae or brownie dessert you typically would see at a diner. So I'm sure the average dessert value per customer is going to be much higher here than any other diner in town. What else does Tony do to help boost that average customer value?"

"Rick, you don't miss much, do you? Well as you noticed Jennifer read off the daily specials and asked us about a daily drink special—both alcoholic and non alcoholic. Tony knows his margins on specific items and he also knows his waste factors. So he designs the specials based on cases of meat and ingredients he can buy for a better price. He does the same thing with his drinks. Then he preps his team and scripts out exactly what they should say at each table—and he incentivizes them for moving the specials. It becomes a whole team sales environment.

"You probably don't hear much about restaurants being sales organizations, but that's exactly what he tells his employees the day he hires them. 'You aren't a part of a diner, you are part of a sales team. And every minute you are selling our wonderful food and service.' As a result his is one of the most profitable restaurants in town, and as I mentioned they are expanding more and more."

"So, I get how a diner can do this, but what about a dentist? I mean Dr. Jim has to struggle with how to get a higher conversion and average transaction value, doesn't he?" Rick asked.

"You might think that, but it's probably because you already mentioned your dentist is comfortable with just cleaning teeth. Jim isn't. And while he cares deeply for all his patients and their well being, he also cares about increasing the value of each patient that comes through his doors.

"So Jim focuses on *all* his services—not just the routine teeth cleaning and check up. Everything from cosmetic dentistry to product sales. You know, those fancy spinny toothbrushes? They're a very high-margin product. Also dental plans, VIP memberships with special hours, and family plans. All are designed to maximize his lifetime patient value and increase each transaction he has with them. The patients love the experience and don't care they are paying much more per visit than with the other dentists in town they drove past to get to his office.

"It's all about creating an experience, so the customer doesn't mind paying a premium... and even enjoys it," Bill stated.

"I can definitely see how these two do that. I need to look at my pricing and figure out what we can do. If nothing else, I now know we can raise our prices right away," said Rick.

"Well, here is one simple strategy, Rick. Raise your prices indiscriminately every quarter. It doesn't have to be much, only 1-2%, but that gives you a cushion each year. Most customers never notice a 1-2% bump. You'll protect your margins and keep the customer happy. There's your simple put-it-into-action-today idea! I did that in the hardware store quarterly—just had it programmed into my calendar to raise prices. Worked great, and our products were at least 2-5% more than our competitors."

Rick wrote that down and tried to scribble a few other notes. He knew he was in for some action soon. He also knew he needed to dedicate some time to work on his business, despite the full week he already had scheduled.

Rick's Notebook:

Date   ·   No.

- SECOND GEAR: CONVERSION

- Raise my Prices!!!

- Package and bundle products

- How can I do this??

- Upsell - - Don't ask
  won't get

Chapter 14

GOOD IS GOOD ENOUGH

 As they finished their Decadent Chocolate Experience, Bill looked at Rick and asked, "So, are you overwhelmed yet?"

"Entirely. And we aren't even halfway through the gears. But don't cheat me on account of me being the thick-skulled one that isn't doing any of this stuff," Rick smiled as he poked fun at himself.

"Rick, please don't feel bad. Understand that you are not alone. Most business owners don't do these things we are discussing. That's why I love my coaching. It's little ideas that go a long way. You see, the big idea is that your business is a machine and there are gears that need working. It's the little ideas—those one or two little nuggets per gear—that can transform your business.

"I know you'll get this going, starting today when you get back to work. Baby steps, Rick. Don't try to do too much, but also don't let yourself get caught up in perfection. Remember that sometimes good is good enough. Not always, but for certain things it's much better to take imperfect action than to let it sit forever."

"Good advice, Bill. Now let's get on to the third gear before Martin calls me and I have to get my car and go back to work," said Rick.

"Okay, I'll get the check and we can visit about the third gear as we walk back over. Jennifer..."

> *Don't try to do too much, but also don't let yourself get caught up in perfection. Remember that sometimes good is good enough.*
>
> *For more resources:*
> *GearedForGrowth.com/Bonus*

Bill waived her down. "Put this on my account and we'll take a to-go box so Rick can share this experience with his kids." Bill made another familiar smile at Rick as he finished talking to Jennifer.

"Bill, you know I can't let you treat me. This is free consulting and now you are paying for lunch? No way. I insist," Rick stammered.

"No, no, no. Rick, this is what I love doing. Keep your money in your wallet and keep learning. Then go back and take action. Implementation is where the profit is, not in checking email," he smiled.

They received their to-go box and Bill signed the check. Rick was also presented with a very nice folder with details about his new VIP All Star Diner pass. It came complete with a story of the origin of the diner and Tony's family and background, as well as a calendar of events, his VIP special savings and perks of being a member, and a very nicely presented coupon for a free appetizer on his next visit. It also contained a brief questionnaire and self-addressed stamped envelope for him to send it back in. The survey allowed them to know in advance what Rick would prefer on his visits to further enhance his dining experience.

It was impressive and impactful. But now Rick knew it was all part of the machine Tony and Bill were working on together. It was exactly the type of experience Rick wanted his customers to have when they left his sign company.

Rick knew if he could start to implement some of these things he could transform his sign company into a better, larger, and more profitable business. He reminded himself of the ambitious goals he'd had when he bought the business and how they had seemed to fade away as he got sucked more and more into daily operations.

This encounter was exactly what Rick needed to boost him forward. He knew he would end up hiring Bill in some capacity, regardless of the cost. This investment would pay him back many times over. And they were only through two of the gears!

Rick couldn't wait to learn more and was anxious to see where the conversation would lead. His excitement was peaking when suddenly his cell phone rang again.

Chapter 15

OPPORTUNITY KNOCKS

"Rick," Brian almost shouted through the phone, "we just got a call from Expotain Health!" He sounded out of breath, almost hyperventilating.

"Rick, I don't know what to do, they need a lot of signs and quick. They said another company really let them down and they called to see what we could do. I need your help! When are you coming back?"

Rick tried to remain calm. Based on what he had just learned, he wanted to think strategically. "Brian, slow down and take a deep breath. How did the conversation go? Did you get all the contact information and details?" Rick knew instantly that his company's phone presence and training had failed the sign company yet again.

"Well, I have his name and phone number. I told him I would have you call him today before the end of day," Brian stated.

Rick glanced at his watch and realized it was only 12:35 pm. He had time to finish up with Bill, get his car, and get back before calling to talk details.

"Brian, do me a favor. Call them back and confirm that I will be in touch before the end of the day. Let them know we are very interested in discussing the details. Tell them I will be back in the office before 2:00 pm and will reach out directly at that point. Thank them and ask when the best time to reach them this afternoon would be. Can you do that?" Rick asked.

"I, I, I think so, Rick. It's just that they are so big. This could be a huge opportunity! Can't you just call them back right now?" Brian asked.

"Brian, I doubt the world will explode before 2:00 pm. It's quite alright if I call them upon my return. I am in a meeting and need to finish before I can return the call. They will understand. And your courtesy call back will further ensure that we are a customer-friendly company who will help them with their needs. Okay, Brian?" Rick asked patiently.

"Okay, boss. I guess I can do that. I really hope this works out."

"It will. And, Brian? Don't guess you can do it, do it. You know this business as well as I do. You can confidently assure them that we are the right place for their business. You'll do great. I'll see you around 2:00 pm," Rick finished and hung up.

Secretly he wanted to rush back, make the call and see how he could win the business of Expotain. They were the leading health care organization in the area. They owned four hospitals and had over fifty off-site facilities. It was exactly the type of company Rick wanted to work with and grow with. He had tried unsuccessfully to reach out to them for years.

Recently he had even asked his network if they knew anyone in that company. He received a few names and requested introductions. He'd followed up with a personal letter to each new contact. Hopefully that was how this call was generated, but he couldn't be sure.

Either way, Rick knew from talking to Bill that creating the right experience was key. If Rick took that call now, he wouldn't be in the right state of mind, or have the right environment to concentrate and give Expotain the best service and phone presence possible.

He looked forward to the chance to secure a new customer—just one of the three ways to grow his business.

Rick's Notebook:

Date

- CALL: EXPOTAIN by 2PM

- Remain calm and talk
  through the situation

Remember the FIRST GEAR!!

Chapter 16

CAPTIVATION

 As Bill and Rick walked back to M&M Garage, Bill began discussing the third gear.

"Alright, Rick, this will put us over the halfway hump through the machine. Third gear is called Captivation. You see, just having a new customer, getting a higher transaction value, and creating a good experience is not always enough to create a captive customer—meaning one who wants to return again and again, and who wants to tell others about you.

"Captivation is all about making sure that after a customer's experience, they are so captivated by your company, they can't wait to tell others and return.

"So, Rick, what are some ways you could further captivate someone who just bought a sign, so they want to talk about you?" Bill asked.

"Well, I don't think I know." Rick seemed puzzled. "I mean we don't really do much at all now."

"Not uncommon, Rick. That's why so few people are captivated by small businesses. One of the first things I would suggest you put in place right away is to say 'Thank You.' Do you do that now?" he asked.

"Well, of course we say thank you when they pick up their sign," Rick clarified almost defensively. "I don't think that's a problem."

"Hmm, well of course you do, Rick. But I imagine a good bit of your business is installing signs or maybe even shipping signs or just delivering signs, right?" Bill asked.

"Ah, of course! Not much gets past you, does it, Bill? Now I see where this is going," Rick admitted slightly deflated.

"Rick, you are probably missing the 'Thank You' on many of your orders. And trust me... sending the invoice doesn't count as thank you." Bill smiled as he stated what seemed obvious, but Rick imagined was a common mistake.

"You see 'Thank You' and someone's first name are probably the three most important words anyone can hear. People love to feel appreciated. And everyone loves to hear their first name, or see it in print. So you have to be sure that every customer *every time* gets thanked and sees or hears their name. Not some generic pre-printed plain-jane thank you postcard—although that's better than nothing!" Bill joked.

"So you have to have a system in place to thank your customers on a regular basis. At our hardware store we called every TB's Team VIP member after each time they made a purchase. I know that sounds crazy, but imagine getting a call from your local hardware store thanking you and asking if your project worked out okay! Unheard of, right? Different than the competitors. That's why we grew. We were captivating our customers."

"But, Bill, how did you do that before you had your call centers in place? I mean you must have had thousands of purchases a day, right?" Rick asked.

"You're exactly right, Rick. We had to outsource it, and that scared me, but it was the only way we could do it at our volume. And TB still does that today. But it's happening, and it's cheaper than mail... *and* it builds a higher level of trust. Now I would anticipate that at your business you don't have thousands of customer transactions per day, right?" Bill asked.

"No, probably only a handful. But we are so busy with the daily activities, how could we ever build in time to call everyone *every time*?" Rick doubted.

"It's a matter of priority, Rick, and a matter of focus. I'm not saying you have to do this on day one. You could just start by sending a pre-printed postcard that says 'Thank You' from you the owner. And remember, you don't have to thank all customers the same every time. It's not a democracy here. You can cherry pick all day long.

Call your highest value customers, but send the others postcards. Don't you want to invest in the customers who have the most potential? I hope so. Pick and choose and thank accordingly.

"Dr. Jim sends thank you gifts to all his new patients at their home. But if they

> *Captivation is all about standing out in a crowded marketplace.*
>
> For more ideas on how you can stand out, visit:
> GearedForGrowthBook.com/Bonus

purchase a product, get cosmetic work, or generate more than a certain transaction value, they get a much nicer package in the mail. He purposefully adds more value to his higher value customers, while still building value for all his customers.

"Captivation is all about standing out in a crowded marketplace. A world that constantly demands the time, attention, and money of your customers. It's not that hard to do, Rick... but so few do it," said Bill.

"Thank You' is just one way to captivate," Bill stated.

They were approaching the garage and walked up to its entrance. Rick noticed something he hadn't paid attention to until his new friend made him more aware.

The garage was so clean it appeared more like a retail establishment than a garage. The windows were clean, the waiting area didn't smell like gas and burnt coffee, and everything inside appeared to enhance the new customer experience.

"So Bill, I don't suppose you work with Martin too, do you?" Rick asked, now seeing the world through his own 'new customer goggles' approach to business.

Rick's Notebook:

Date · No.

THIRD GEAR: CAPTIVATION

- say thank you more
- How do I stand out??

Do I WOW?

Lots of choices in our market

Chapter 17

ANOTHER MACHINE STUDENT

"Rick, before I answer that question, tell me why you ask," Bill said. "Specifically, based on what you have learned, what would give you such an idea?" He cracked a slight smile.

Rick began, "Well for one thing, it's the cleanest entry and waiting area I have ever seen at a locally owned garage. I mean, maybe you see it at the big box stores, but almost never at a locally owned garage. They're typically dumps, smell like engines, and have magazines plastered all over the waiting room tables. Old coffee with white Styrofoam cups and a few candy machines that require money to get anything out of.

"So Martin's waiting room atmosphere instantly changed that feel. I know it's only because of my 'new customer goggles' I even realize it. I've been coming here for years since our car broke down and the tow truck brought us here. I never really put much thought into why I chose to keep coming back, even though it's on the other side of town. But now I'm starting to realize... Martin has a success and profits machine!" Rick stated confidently.

"I remember thinking it was odd when he sat us down and did an interview when we first came in. Then I received a packet from him in the mail. It's all becoming clear now! It contained a trash bag for my car, a scent pack for the glove compartment, and coupons for my next visit."

Rick's mind was reeling. He hadn't thought too much of it at the time, but now that he knew about Bill's "5 gears" it was becoming crystal clear why he had kept returning to M&M Garage for service.

"Shortly after that I received mailings from Martin directly, thanking me and also offering to make me part of his VIP customer group. I thought it was crazy at the time, but now I see he was working on the second of the three laws—the second gear—Conversion!"

Rick barreled on, enthusiasm in his every word. "First gear was in full action when he sat my wife and I down to interview us about the repair, and clearly third gear kicked in when we received the package in the mail. And then after that we even got a thank you note from Martin." Rick was talking faster, now clearly excited at his revelations. "Wow Bill, is there anyone in this town you don't work with?"

"Ha, Rick! I only wish I was that good. But congratulations on your ability to quickly learn and decipher how other businesses are using the machine to tweak each gear and be more successful. Unfortunately, this will develop into a healthy sickness... you will always be analyzing, thinking of ways to improve the gears in every business you visit.

"And remember, we are just barely over halfway!" said Bill.

"But you are a quick learner and despite us only touching on a few of the ways to use these gears, you are already spotting successes early. The next step is putting those into practice in your own business. It can easily be done. You just have to carve out the time and make it a priority to work on each gear... one at a time."

"So how do I keep from wanting to rush into it all at once, Bill? I'm concerned because... well... now I think my business stinks!" Rick exclaimed, half laughing half serious.

> *What you've already done got you to where you are. But it's what you do next that will take your business where you truly want it to be.*
>
> To Get More Ideas Visit GearedForGrowth.com/Bonus

"Slow down there, Rick. Don't forget that you have a successful business. What you've already done got you to where you are. But it's what you do next that will take your business where you truly want it to be.

"Remember two things I said earlier: First, implementation equals profit. Just keep taking baby steps. And second, inspect what you expect.

"You don't have to reinvent the wheel. Just start by making little changes we discuss and you will see massive results over time. As long as you continue to implement—and continue to enforce the changes you make.

"Now do you want to learn the fourth and fifth gears, or what?" Bill asked jokingly.

Chapter 18

CULTIVATION

They walked back into the waiting room of Martin's garage and sat down on the nice leather couches in one corner. They were on the opposite side of the retail counter, away from the noise of the phones, customers coming and going, and the large flat screen TV other waiting customers were watching while enjoying complimentary snacks and beverages.

Bill settled down into the nice couch and stretched his arms and legs for a moment. Then he began again by asking a question to Rick. "What do you think is the most important asset in your business?"

Rick paused and thought for a minute. "I know that whatever I say is probably not the right answer. I'm trying to think with my 'machine' head on, but I'm still coming up empty. I guess I'd have to say it's my employees... but that's not really an asset, is it?"

Bill smiled, "Well, at least you're thinking in new ways. That's actually a common answer and they are a valuable asset—but not the most valuable. You see, Rick, if you believe that every customer has value—and you believe you can *increase* that value—then the most important asset in your business is not just your customer list, but your *relationship* with your customer list.

> *The purpose of a customer is not to get a sale. The purpose of a sale is to get a customer.*

"If indeed that's the most important asset, then you can manage it like an asset... to get a real, measurable, and valuable return on that asset.

"A big mistake most business owners make is that they think the purpose of a customer is to get a sale. But, the reverse is actually true. You see the purpose of a sale or transaction should actually be to get and increase the value of a customer.

"Did you follow that? Because most business owners think in terms of growth—sell more stuff, get more customers. They neglect the real reason for selling more stuff. It should be to get more customers in order to increase your best asset—the relationship with those customers—and then to increase the value of those assets. Does that make sense?"

"I think so," Rick stammered, "but I'm still confused. If the purpose of a sale is to get and increase the value of a customer, then where or how do I increase the value of the asset? Is that the relationship with the customer? Isn't that where you said the real money is?"

"You're really catching on, Rick. Great question," Bill assured. "Remember that having a relationship with your customers is part of what helps you get more sales from them. Generating a sale is still a relationship builder, because each time you encounter that customer you have a chance to build the relationship through great service and great products... and to provide an amazing follow-up experience.

"That leads us to the fourth gear, Cultivation.

"According to the dictionary, 'cultivate' means to grow or raise under conditions you can control. So likewise, Cultivation as the fourth gear is where you grow or raise the value of your customers under conditions you control. You can't control someone's wallet or need for services, but you can control their behaviors and mindset so they value you more, and in turn become more valuable to you. That's what the fourth gear is all about... growing and raising the value of your current customers—the Cultivation of great customer relationships.

"So how do we go about doing this? Well, let's go back to our examples of Jim and Tony. Dr. Jim is a great example of cultivation in action. Each month he sends out a printed monthly newsletter to all his patients. That might sound old-school and even expensive in this digital 'free and cheap age,' but it's actually by far his number one marketing activity, consistently producing results for him."

"Really?" Rick blurted out. "A printed newsletter? That does sound old school. My business is different. Everyone prefers email these days," Rick stated confidently.

Bill glanced at his watch and chuckled. "I was wondering how long it would take you to say that!" He laughed loudly and slapped Rick on the knee.

Rick was confused. He had no idea what he'd said to cause this reaction.

Rick's Notebook:

Date · No.

FOURTH GEAR: CULTIVATION

- Purpose of a sale is to
  Get a customer

- Lifetime value of a
  Customer?? Do I know
  this number?   CALCULate
- start a monthLy printed
  newsLetter

89

Chapter 19

MY BUSINESS IS DIFFERENT

 "Bill, I have to be honest. I have no idea why you're laughing. What did I say that was so funny?" Rick asked defensively. "Weren't we talking about a printed monthly newsletter and Cultivation?"

"Ha," Bill exclaimed. "Why yes, we were. But let me explain why what you said offhand is the cancer of successful entrepreneurs.

"Right after you told me newsletters were old school, you said four little words that in my coaching, are as bad as a four-letter curse word. Do you remember what they were?" Bill peered at him intently.

"Honestly, I don't remember, Bill. Your laugh and knee slap threw me off. I lost all train of thought. But now I really want to know. I certainly don't need a cancer in my business."

"The four most dangerous words are: MY BUSINESS IS DIFFERENT.

"Those four little words have cost my clients more money than I ever made in my career... more money than the gross sales of TB's Hardware combined over the years. I mean that more sincerely than you can possibly imagine."

"What do you mean, Bill. My business *is* different. We send digital proofs all the time. Our website drives prospects to online communications, and we use social media to showcase our jobs and successes all the time. My customers are just too busy to read a printed paper newsletter. My business has to be different. Surely a print newsletter wouldn't work. I mean my customers are business people, not consumers going to a dentist, you

> *The four most dangerous words are: MY BUSINESS IS DIFFERENT*

know?" But the more Rick talked, the less sure he became. He realized Bill was very sincere. Maybe he'd just backed himself into a corner.

"Rick, you're not entirely off in your thinking, but if you allow it to stay and linger, it *will* become a cancer to your business. You see, most entrepreneurs only look at their business through their own perspective. It's the easiest and most convenient way to do it. But when we take off the blinders and let others examine our business—and give us their most successful ideas—that's when we truly have breakthroughs.

"The phrase 'My business is different' is the blinder that must be removed. Sadly, many of my clients, and most small business owners, never want to remove that blinder. Here's why: it's hard. It takes lots of thinking, lots of testing and lots of energy. It's just too hard for most people. They want to maintain status quo, yet still grow. And that's just not possible.

"Do you know the definition of insanity, Rick?" Bill asked. "It's doing the same thing over and over again, but expecting different results.

"By that definition, most business owners are certainly insane!" he proclaimed.

Rick adjusted his position on the love seat across from Bill, moving to avoid the uncomfortable state of mind. "Well, I'm definitely guilty of that, Bill. I guess I'm insane. So how do I remove the blinders and keep myself from saying 'My business is different'? What's the cancer cure?" Rick was now genuinely seeking wisdom.

"Rick, it takes time, but here are two quick ideas to help. First, because you run a sign shop, I want you to make a sign that says 'NO, MY BUSINESS IS *NOT* DIFFERENT'. And then I want you to hang it up and read it everyday!"

Bill laughed, but Rick knew he was serious. He could make a little sign to hang above his office door where he'd be sure to read it everyday. Rick made a note to do that right away.

"The second way I have found effective is to mastermind with other successful business owners.

Now I know that word sounds all "hocus pocusey" but it was actually a phrase made popular by Napoleon Hill. Do you know who that was?" Bill asked.

"I think I've heard the name, but I'm not sure," Rick admitted guiltily.

"Don't worry, you're not alone. He was the author of *Think and Grow Rich*, a book written in 1937, after the Great Depression, that is still just as applicable today as it was then. One of his key points is the power of masterminding.

"It's really just getting together with like-minded individuals to see how you can share ideas to help each other. But when facilitated properly and organized with specific purposes in mind, it can help you grow your business leaps and bounds.

"Let me explain. Let's say you have a problem with expenses creeping up on you. You've looked at it every which way and tried to cut things, but still you're up against a wall. You could bring this topic up in discussion at a mastermind meeting, describe the problem and what you have tried, and pose a question to the group. Each person can then ask questions and offer their advice based on your answers. Now you have multiple ideas how to control or attack the problem—several of which you probably never even considered—just because you were only looking at it through your own perspective."

"Wow, I never even thought of that! But I guess that's the point, huh? I've never heard of that type of group, though. Is that strange?" Rick asked.

"Not at all. They're out there, but the key is finding the right group. It's usually best to find one that is either industry-specific or that is run by someone who understands business well and who you can relate to based on what you know about that person and their experience.

"These masterminds aren't cheap, but they're worth every penny invested. The group I run consistently has high retention. Our members often claim that one idea paid for their entire year's membership. It's all about the power of using other peoples' minds to help you get to the best solution.

"These two ideas are the best way to keep yourself from saying 'My business is different' and falling into the fatal cancer of not growing.

"Well, we got off track a bit, Rick. Let's get back to Cultivation and newsletters..."

Rick's Notebook:

Date · No.

- Look into a mastermind

- READ: Think and grow Rich
  - Napoleon Hill

Chapter 20

WHY USE MAIL

"So as I was saying, Rick, Dr. Jim uses his monthly printed newsletter to do a number of things. The ultimate goal though is to grow and raise the value of his current customers.

"His newsletter seeks to grow the value of his customers by getting more referrals, offering specials, entertaining them so they look for his mailings and want to read them, and finally showcasing high-value patients and how they were successful in their treatments.

"Just those four items alone are worth their weight in gold. And if he only did email to communicate with them, he would never see the same level of returns as he does from his newsletter. But here's the kicker, Rick, he emails it too! So he doesn't fight the current trends, he embraces them. He just also maintains what he knows works and gets received— the United States Postal Service!"

"Maybe you are right there, Bill. What are the current open rates of emails these days?" Rick asked.

"Well, I read a lot, and I see different figures all the time, but I'd say that the average for a business is probably only about 13%[1]" Bill stated. "And that can range from as low as 6% to as high as 34% depending on the industry. But any way you slice it, that's less than one out of every four people who actually reads your emails. Not my choice when it comes to important information used to grow or raise the value of my clients... and *their* clients.

"Are you starting to see what I mean here, Rick?" Bill asked. "I send a monthly free newsletter to my entire database of prospects, as well as a newsletter specifically for my paid clients that has much more content and a little different focus. I practice what I preach, my friend.

"I and Dr. Jim and even Tony, to his VIP clients, use a monthly printed newsletter to cultivate our best asset—a relationship with our customers.

"But there are other ways too, you know," Bill continued.

"Mr. Baylor," a voice clearly called from behind them. "Might I have a word with you about your vehicle? So sorry to interrupt your great conversation."

"Sure thing," Rick answered as he rose and walked over to the professionally dressed woman holding a

---

[1] 2015 Constant Contact Email Open Rates Comparison by Industry Chart -
http://support2.constantcontact.com/articles/FAQ/2499#Comparison

binder with Rick's name and vehicle info printed on the cover.

"Mr. Baylor, my name is Stacey and I'm assisting Mr. Martin with your vehicle today. It looks like they will be finishing up in about fifteen minutes so I wanted to see if we could review your investment today and get you express checked out so you can leave as soon as your vehicle is ready. Would that be okay with you?" she asked politely.

"Sure thing, let me just tell Bill I'll be right back," he explained.

"Bill, let me see what gear Martin is working on right now while Stacey checks me out. I'll be right back. You've been talking so much the drinks are on me... right over there at the free snack and beverage counter," Rick smiled and laughed as he walked over to the desk to review his account.

Rick's Notebook:

Date · No.

- Use a newsLetter to:

1 Increase value of
   Customers
2 Get referrals
3 Entertain
4 showcase high doLLar
   projects/successes

Chapter 21

GROW THE CUSTOMER

"Alright, I'm back, Bill. Now we need to wrap up gear four and get to gear five before my express check-out gets me the heck out of here... so I can start implementing!" Rick said with a big grin of excitement.

"No doubt you will be implementing and seeing success soon, Rick. Let's wrap up the fourth gear—Cultivation.

"We already discussed the monthly printed newsletter, but how else can we grow or raise the value of a customer? A newsletter focuses highly on the relationship side and also leads to more sales, but what about the direct selling aspect of growing the value of a customer? How can you do that?" Bill asked Rick.

"Well, I know in Martin's case—and in what I just paid for—he sends me offers in the mail all the time. And not just coupons, but offers tied directly to a story or an event going on that are time-sensitive. I have to see what the offer is and how I can use it because it's not always just money off or a percentage discount.

"He's very creative in how he makes offers. And now that I think of it, Bill, even in how he presents those offers to me. I just got a birthday card in the mail for my car! Seems silly, but when I realized a year had passed and I needed to get my car inspected, I found the mailer included a coupon for a free inspection for my car's birthday so it didn't feel so old! Clever, *and* useful. I'm here, and guess what, the inspection's free, but I'm several hundred dollars lighter because of the other work that had to be done at the same time in order to pass inspection!"

"Perfect, Rick. See how fast you are learning? It won't be long until you are teaching the class!" Bill snickered.

"You are exactly right, Rick. Direct mail is a key component of cultivating your customers. You have to make offers to them. Over time people just forget who they used for a product or service. Even if the experience was great, we are all so overwhelmed with advertising and media, we forget things.

"It's your job as the owner to cultivate them so well they can't stop thinking about you.

"In our hardware store we used to send all types of things to our TB's Team VIP program members. We sent emails, we sent birthday cards, we sent reports of what they bought for future reference, we sent offers, we even made calls to check in when they hadn't been in for a while. All to help cultivate and grow and raise the value of those customers.

"Tony sends offers to both entice new clients to come in, and then even more offers to VIP members to get them to return. He knows them by name and tries to learn more each visit so he can increase the frequency in which they return. He knows one frequently returning patron is far more valuable than four new first-time patrons if he doesn't capture information. His entire goal is to get his VIP members to come in to the diner at least eight times a year. His most valuable clients come in over 75 times a year! They are rewarded, recognized and praised.

"His value per patron far exceeds anyone else in this town, and it's obvious why. He cultivates them regularly.

"It's the power of the machine, Rick. The power of what you will have in just a short time," Bill explained.

"Oh man, I certainly hope you are right, Bill. Now let's keep moving. I only have about ten minutes left and I need the last gear and some type of closure on this whole thing!" Rick said.

Rick's Notebook:

Date · No.

- Use offers to cultivate

- Direct Mail works!!

- Build valuable Customers
   1 Returning regular
   Customer is better than
   4 new ones?
Returning is more valuable
And cheaper!

Chapter 22

MACHINE RECAP

"Well, Rick, it's hard to think we have almost covered this whole machine thing and it's not even dinner time. When I teach this in a seminar it's typically two days! So you are really getting the crash course, my friend!" Bill joked.

"And I greatly appreciate it, Bill. Let's talk Gear 5, the last one, right? I bet it's super exciting!" Rick said almost like a child awaiting candy.

"Calm down, Rick. Fifth gear is very important, but it's certainly not the sexiest. Remember I told you there were five gears and each one needed to be maintained, tweaked and developed individually for the whole machine to work at it's best?

"Your goal is not to judge which one is more important than any other... it's to always be tweaking, improving and measuring the gears and how they are working together. That's what a mechanic does, and you are becoming a mechanic of a success and profits machine." Bill stated.

"So before we dive into the last gear, let's do a quick recap of the four other gears. They are much more operational in nature than the fifth gear.

Bill outlined them aloud while Rick took notes.

1st Gear – Conversation: Remember it's always happening and you never know who could be your next client. The Phones are one of the most important parts of this gear.

2nd Gear – Conversion: Getting the most out of each transaction is key to growth. Focus on raising prices, bundling services and products, and upselling at time of purchase.

3rd Gear – Captivation: You have to captivate them quickly after their experience. Be sure to say thank you and show up after the initial transaction.

4th Gear – Cultivation: You can grow and raise the value of a customer with things you control—like them giving referrals, taking you up on an offer and coming to see you more often.

Now, with those four gears in mind, let's shift to the fifth and final gear—Cash Flow.

Chapter 23

CASH FLOW

"Cash flow?" Rick said confused, "Really? That's the fifth gear? But all the other ones were so fun and exciting. Who wants to talk about cash flow?"

"I warned you, Rick, but everyone needs to talk about cash flow. You see the number one reason businesses fail, or worse never grow and are unhappy, is cash flow.

"Most business owners don't know their numbers, don't have good cash flow, and get themselves in a situation where they stop doing the other four gears because they simply don't have enough cash.

"So yes, Cash Flow is the fifth gear and while not as sexy, it's crucial to the success of a growing business.

"Rick, I learned early in my first business before TB's that cash was very important. Everyone sees gross sales and thinks a business owner is rich! They might even see *net* profits and think a business owner is rich. But no business owner I ever knew was rich on paper without having cash in the bank.

"It's a common problem and especially with growing businesses. They think the cash will come simply because they have growing sales and profits. But employees don't work for IOUs and the bank won't take them either—and the IRS *certainly* won't take them. So cash is critical to the success of your business.

"I'll share a secret, Rick," Bill leaned in closer. "My first business failed because of cash flow. We grew too fast and too much and the cash ran out. Lots of people owed me money, but expenses came faster than cash did. I had to declare bankruptcy and close down a high six-figure business... all because I couldn't pay the bills.

"It was sad, but Rick, I learned my lesson and now I teach it so others don't have to experience it. Cash flow is vital to your growth."

Rick looked down at the ground like a dog caught after making a mess in the house, tail between its legs. "Bill, it's like you're reading my mind. Cash is always a struggle and right now I'm trying to figure out how to fund payroll on Friday, even when we are growing.

"I hope this gear gives me some guidance so I can stop feeling sorry for myself and fix my problem," Rick admitted ashamedly.

Chapter 24

CREATE MORE CASH

"Rick, you've heard me say this before, so I'll say it again. You're not alone. It's okay... but it's not okay if you can't pay your bills. That's what we want to fix and discuss with the fifth gear. I think we can come up with some ideas to really help.

"First things first. Do you require a deposit on every job you produce at your sign shop?" Bill asked.

"Well, uh, it depends. I mean, yes and no. I mean, sometimes, I guess?" Rick was clearly caught in a situation of not knowing how to answer.

"In my first business, Rick, we manufactured custom hose fittings. Not an exciting product, but a profitable and needed one. We would accept orders for 100,000 fittings and not require a deposit. That meant I was fronting all the cash for the job then waiting to get paid. It sucked cash faster than a Texas Tornado sucks up dust bunnies.

"It doomed us to trouble. So that's an easy one, start requiring a deposit on all jobs, and whenever possible, especially with small companies, payment all up front.

"Secondly, do you have a routine and automatic savings plan for cash reserves?" he asked Rick.

"No, I don't, but I'm not sure I know what you mean," Rick admitted.

"It's always a pain to go to the bank and ask for a line of credit, and their terms might not suit you, and certainly won't suit your timeframe. You need to create your own internal line of credit by incrementally and regularly taking chunks of money and putting them into a savings account. When we started TB's it was only $50 a week until we could raise it up. Eventually we had our own $1,000,000 internal line of credit. Seems like a lot, but it started with one store and $50 a week. It adds up quickly and we gradually increased the weekly amount contributed to the savings account. It all came from little amounts weekly that we didn't miss.

"Start saving a little at a time and try not to touch it until you absolutely have to. Then put it back as quickly as you can. In good times and in bad times. It will help save your skin when you need it, and it's a lot cheaper than the bank's money!" he smiled.

"Lastly, manage your cash. Don't pay bills earlier than you have to, don't commit too much to one thing, and always always *always* know exactly how much money you have in the bank, after all outstanding checks and items that have not cleared. You can't run a business if you don't know how much cash you have in the bank.

"We used a simple spreadsheet to manage this, but you have to have a way to know the balance in the checking account after checks you have written would clear.

"The last thing I want to hear is that Rick's business went under because he couldn't pay his bills. Especially when I know that once you implement these five gears and have your own success and profits machine, it's going to take off like a rocket!" Bill exclaimed with confidence.

"All great ideas, Bill. I know I need to work on this fifth gear to get my situation under control. It just always seems like there is never enough cash."

"Every small business owner runs into this on a regular basis. It's all relative. To you $1,000 might not seem like enough, but to someone else the figure might be $100,000. But they most likely have expenses that could suck that dry just as quickly as your $1,000. Just work on these three systems and always watch the cash flow.

"Without this fifth gear, your machine is not moving anywhere, guaranteed!

"Oh and I almost forgot..."

"Rick!" someone yelled from the entrance.

A middle-aged professionally dressed smiling woman approached them.

Rick's Notebook:

Date · No.

- **FIFTH GEAR: CASH FLOW**
- Get Deposits on ALL Jobs
- Know your cash balance

To download resources and tools to help you grow, visit: www.GearedForGrowthBook.com/Bonus

Chapter 25

OIL CHANGE, MY TREAT

"Rick, it's so good to see you. I thought you never got out of that sign company pumping out all those signs for us," she said in an assuredly excited voice.

"Well hi there, Susan," Rick said politely. He stood and gave her a friendly welcoming hug. "What brings you to this side of town and M&M Garage?" Rick asked.

"I have some meetings this afternoon and we are touring a new facility that we might be purchasing soon... more sign work for you!" she said with a big smile. "And I needed to get my oil changed while I was waiting for my next meeting. How's the crew? I haven't seen Brian in a while. I've been busy and haven't been able to make most of the recent installs."

"The crew is good, and thank you for your continued business. I trust we are doing a good job taking care of your needs?" Rick inquired.

"Rick, you and your team always do a great job, and if you didn't, I'd tell you," she stated.

"Well, I appreciate that, but I have to always ask. You know we want to take great care of you and be sure you are happy with the service and the product. In fact, is there anything we need to improve on that might make your life easier or our dealings simpler?" Rick inquired again.

"Rick, you always do great work and your team is doing a great job. Nothing really comes to mind..." she paused for just one minute, slightly squinted one eye and tilted her head to the left just a little, clearly thinking.

"Oh, actually, just one idea that might help. If you could just shoot me an email or a text message when Brian or your other installer is coming to a site. Just gives me a heads-up as to when work is being completed. Sometimes the uppity guys at a few of the sites get upset if I don't know when someone was there. Other than that, you guys rock!" she said again with a smile and confidence.

"Thank you, Susan, I appreciate that, and I'll definitely talk to the team and make sure we add that to our job checklist. I tell you what, I'm paying for your oil change and I'll even tell Martin to throw in new wipers and fluid checks. I'll take care of it." Rick waived to Stacey, the M&M Garage Concierge, to make arrangements.

"Stop, Rick! Are you kidding me? You're not paying for my car repairs!" She punched him in the arm in a friendly way.

"I insist," Rick replied. "Just sit back and relax and know that we appreciate your business and will keep working hard for you. Honestly, it's the least I can do."

"Well, thank you. Maybe I should tell him to throw in four new tires on your bill, too," she said and smiled, again laughing. "You're awesome. And look for some emails later today with more orders for the site you just completed."

She walked away and talked it over with Stacey. Stacey pulled up her appointment on the computer and walked her to the refreshment zone to make sure she was comfortable. Susan was always working and pulled out her bag to review items for her next meeting.

It was a small price for Rick to pay. Susan was the facilities director for a local retirement community. They had multiple locations throughout the state and she was consistently ordering signs for their communities.

She was great to work with and Rick was always working to find more people like Susan—and also to make sure Susan and her whole company knew who he was and how he could help them. He had focused on retirement communities a few years prior and had success in gaining most of the local retirement community businesses in some way or another.

Rick made his way back to the table and smiled, "Sorry for the interruption, Bill. She is one of our best customers. Nice to see her out in public, and thanks to you I thought I would take care of her bill here at the garage as a way of saying 'Thank You'."

Bill smiled and Rick could tell he had something important to say.

Chapter 26

MAKE IT A SYSTEM

 "Rick, that was one of the finest things I have seen in quite some time. Do you realize what you just did?" Bill asked intently.

"Well, I guess I cultivated the relationship a little more, right? Fourth gear?" Rick said tentatively.

"Yes, but you did it in a very strategic manner. Great pick-up of the fourth gear! See, you are a fast learner," Bill laughed.

"What was so magical about that process was that it is a system. Whether you realize it or not, that is a cultivation system you can use, teach, and implement in your business... and track. Do you know what that system was?" Bill asked.

"No idea, I'm just glad I got the right gear when I answered!" Rick smiled and realized he was catching on.

"Let me show you how to make it a system you can repeat. You did four key things there that you can do regularly and track.

1) You thanked her.

2) You asked her how you were doing as a vendor.
3) You asked her what needed improvement.
4) You showed appreciation through a gift.

"Let's look at those four things quickly. Understand that they're a key part of fourth gear we didn't even touch on.

"First, you said 'Thank you.' Do you know how many times I spend money and no one says 'Thank you'? Too many. We touched on this briefly already, so that's not new to you.

"Second, you asked her how you were doing. Most businesses never ask, or they just send an email survey. People are busy... and without proper incentives you can forget about getting any feedback through an email survey.

"Third, you asked her how you can improve. This is a sign of honesty, integrity, and vulnerability. What if she would have told you a horror story? Or what if she would have said, 'I really like you, but your team keeps making mistakes'? She could have said anything, and you were okay with that... because you followed up by saying you would add it to your process.

"It takes a lot of courage and wisdom to ask for what you need to get better on. Many people don't like to hear criticism. It builds the relationship, though, because most consumers just want their voice to be heard. You gave the opportunity for her to state an opinion. Listening is so valuable in a world of self-centeredness. Great job.

"Finally, you showed appreciation through an unexpected gift. That's great! I don't know that I would even have thought of that one. I'm sure Martin will find a way to easily let you take care of her oil change, and he might even find a way to make this a natural process for his other business clients—to let them prepay for their customers to come in for maintenance work.

"Martin might owe *you* dinner for that one!" Bill said with a smile. Somehow Rick knew Bill would pass along that idea to Martin and add yet another nugget of business-producing advice to the garage's revenue stream. It would even work for both the dentist and the diner.

Rick was amazed, "I never would have thought to make that into a process, yet if I write it out and use it as I make calls to other top customers, it would really help cultivate those relationships. I need to be sure to start that. Even if I only do it for my top ten customers once a quarter, that's just 40 more calls than I'm making now. Who knows what I'll learn? Wow, that's a big one! Thanks, Bill."

"That's what the learning process is all about, Rick. Fine-tuning each gear and adding ideas to it so it runs smoother and faster. Then making those successful ideas into a system so it happens everytime, without fail," Bill said.

"Now, I left you hanging on fifth gear with one of the most important items right as Susan was coming over to greet you."

Chapter 27

GET YOUR MONEY

 "I'm in suspense, Bill. What is the most important part of the Cash Flow fifth gear?" Rick asked, moving to the edge of his seat.

"It doesn't apply to every business, but for your business and for TB's contractor accounts, it was the accounts receivable. People who are making money off of your money. It is a part of business, but it's a deadly part on your end if not managed properly.

"Some simple ways to help manage accounts receivable include first and foremost always knowing how much is owed to you. This is your future cash line. You want to know what your cash might look like in 30, 45, or even 60 days.

"You also need to know where each account stands. As soon as someone hits 30 days, they need to be reminded of their bill. If they get to 60 days, you need to have a formal call-system in place. And if they happen to get past 90 days, do whatever you have to do to get that money into your hands.

"Rick, as you mentioned, there never seems to be enough cash, but what if you had 50% of your accounts receivable right now? How would that change your cash position?" Bill had a serious look on his face.

"It would make a world of difference. I'm sure I could find ways to *spend* it," he grinned, "but it sure would help me sleep better," Rick said.

"Exactly, and yet so few business owners make this a part of their weekly routine and schedule. I'm not suggesting you do it all, or all at once, but in the beginning you may have to. It's about having a process and system in place to make sure it doesn't get out of hand. We used to set goals for each past due bucket—we never wanted our 'past 90 days' to exceed 5% of the total owed to us. Then we set goals for 'past 60 days' and 'past 30 days'. It is just so important.

"I have worked with a number of my clients on improving their accounts receivable and each one said it was a game changer. The mindset of the team went from being 'bill sender' to 'cash collector'. You don't want people just sending invoices... you want them getting checks!" Bill said.

"When you get back to the shop, Rick, run a report and put it in your calendar to make those 'past 90' and 'past 60-day' calls yourself. You won't regret it."

Rick's Notebook:

Date · No.

- Run Accts. Receivable Report

Manage My Receivables!!

- what is my follow up system?

**To download resources and tools to help you grow,
visit: www.GearedForGrowthBook.com/Bonus**

Chapter 28

CHIEF BUSINESS TECHNICIAN

 "Mr. Baylor, your vehicle is ready," Stacey said calmly and politely, standing near the two men on the comfortable couches.

"Well Bill, just in the knick of time! I guess I have to get back to my business and see how I can put some of this to work," Rick said.

"I don't know how to even begin to thank you. Can I at least have your address or your card so I can know how to get in touch with you?" Rick asked.

"Sure thing, Rick, and the pleasure was all mine. I love helping other business owners. And more importantly I love learning more about others' businesses. I enjoyed our time together and I hope we can continue the conversations in the future." Bill gave Rick a confident smile and a firm handshake.

"Best of luck to you, Rick. You have what it takes. You just have to get those gears in motion. Take baby steps, but keep moving. It won't be long before you are the one highlighting your successes to others."

Bill handed Rick his business card, turned, and walked toward the door to exit.

Rick was confused because he thought Bill was waiting on his own vehicle repair.

Rick made his way over to the concierge station to finish up with Stacey. He asked, "Can I take care of Mr. Burchess' bill today?"

Stacey smiled and replied, "Mr. Burchess was not having any work done today. He had a meeting with Mr. Martin this morning and he just loves relaxing in the waiting room after their meetings and enjoying a cup of coffee while reading the magazines. It's his monthly routine when he comes for their business coaching session."

Wow, Rick thought. *He took all that time with me, and wasn't even waiting on his vehicle? He even bought me lunch!*

Was this all real, or was I just dreaming? Rick thought.

I really have to sit down and process some of this before I get back into the office and get attacked by the daily grind.

Rick glanced at Bill's card and was surprised to see his title: "Chief Business Technician."

Fitting for a discussion of a success and profits machine for businesses. He loved the tagline under Bill's name: "Gearing Your Business For Growth."

Rick loaded up his car and headed back to the office, knowing he had a wild adventure ahead of him. He wanted his own success machine... and after his conversation with Bill, he did indeed feel "geared for growth."

Chapter 29

HEALTHY RESULTS

"Thanks for all the work you do for us, Rick. You and your team are top notch and one of—if not the best—vendor relationship we have at Expotain Health. I wish all my vendors were as reliable and great as you are. In fact, you're not even a vendor to me, you're a trusted advisor." David walked out the door with a package of signs he had just paid for, after placing another order for several more signs.

David was the Director of marketing for Expotain Health. He had become a customer of Rick's just six months earlier, primarily because his previous sign vendor let him down. He had needed something quickly. Rick remembered that day sitting in the diner with Bill Burchess taking the call from Brian about the need that David and Expotain had.

A lot had changed in just six months. Rick could hardly believe it had been that long since he'd learned how to turn his business into a success and profits machine.

In just six short months, Rick had been busy implementing pieces of each gear into his own business. The results were already starting to show. The first of which was returning David's call after that meeting with Bill—and having much more confidence to be in control rather than acting like he needed the job, despite knowing the impact Expotain could have on their bottom line.

Expotain became a great customer for Rick, and was quickly moving to the top of their customer list after only six months of working together. It was the perfect match.

One of the key implementations Rick was most proud of was fixing his phones. He knew he had a problem but had no way of realizing the impact the phones had been having on his business. Taking the call on his cell phone from Brian that day with Bill—right in the middle of a conversation about the first gear—was like divine inspiration for him.

Rick spent hours working with his team on how to answer the phones best. He consistently coached them and made sure his intake form was being used properly to ensure that no one slipped through the cracks. As a result, their number of contacts in the database had risen drastically in those six short months.

His number of new clients had already doubled over the prior year, and new client sales were triple what they had been the prior six months. All because his team fielded the phones better.

Rick never would have imagined the impact better phone service—with a purpose—would have on his business. The numbers proved it, and the best part was, it didn't cost him anything.

The other key change Rick made regarding first gear was his website. He had a nice website, but it wasn't converting any leads or customers.

Rick designed two key calls to action—a free report on how to increase sales using the visual appearance of one's business, and a $50 New Customer savings pass.

The home page clearly directed visitors to those two key things, followed closely by "Call Us." Rick knew if the phones were fixed, he could drive more calls. He simultaneously increased the amount he was investing to drive web traffic because now he had a way to monitor its success and measure its growth and return on investment.

Rick was thrilled with the results of just improving his first gear.

Rick also joined Bill's Platinum Success Group. It was a big stretch for him, but he knew it would pay dividends well beyond the price of entry. He held up to his own internal promise that Bill was the way to go—no matter what it cost him to invest in the program.

Rick was changing the way he did business and now—teamed with Bill and his group—Rick felt the future was brighter than ever before.

Chapter 30
ONE THAT REALLY WORKED

Another year went by and Rick continued to implement new ideas. Sales continued to increase and Rick's business was now up over 65% from the prior year.

New customers were coming, old customers were returning, and existing customers were spending more than ever before.

Rick had carefully made his way through all five gears and implemented new ideas. Now he was consistently tweaking those systems and always testing fresh concepts.

The biggest return on investment came through the one idea he felt was most ridiculous from his early lunch encounter with Bill: the monthly printed newsletter.

Rick finally started and faithfully produced a monthly printed newsletter for the past 12 months. He couldn't believe the number of customers who commented on it, the amount of his own newsletters he noticed still sitting around when he went out on cultivation calls, or the number of new customers who engaged through the monthly puzzle. It was amazing.

It seemed like just about everyone read his newsletter. Something he felt would be so archaic and turned into trash consistently kept his customers engaged and kept him cultivating relationships that mattered.

Rick's cash flow had greatly improved and his systems for collections, deposits, and knowing where he was financially were in full motion. It was an entirely different feeling each day on his way into work.

Rick couldn't wait for Bill's group calls each month, and the in-person masterminds were some of the most anticipated events of the year for him. Thanks to implementing his success machine, he was able to turn those in-person meetings—many times located around the country—into vacations for either his whole family or just him and his wife. It had truly transformed his business.

But the most exciting part was still to come...

Chapter 31

THE STAR OF THE SHOW

"Welcome, everyone, to the 'Geared for Growth' podcast. I'm Neal Myers, your host, and today we have an amazing show that will get you motivated, get you in action, and give you ideas you can take to the bank." Neal Myers was a part of Bill's coaching team who ran interviews for the monthly podcast.

"This month I not only have the man, the myth, the legend—Bill Burchess, himself—but a very special guest that Bill is personally going to talk with about his huge success to tell us how he achieved it in such a short amount of time.

"Folks, this is the stuff you are looking for. There is no secret to success, but this interview will show you how to implement the right things, the right way, to get to success fast.

"So without further delay, here is your Chief Business Technician and 'Geared For Growth' expert—Bill Burchess!!"

The intro music played and faded out as the interview began.

"Thank you, Neal. You are right that this interview is special for me. Our listeners will walk away with lots of great ideas and value from this podcast today.

"I want to first remind you that becoming 'geared for growth' is a process. It's a system just like the ones we teach you to implement. It takes time and it takes effort—but it rewards with freedom, fun, and fortune when executed regularly.

"The core five gears are fundamentals, but require consistent attention and tweaking. It's when we get too comfortable that we lose traction and slow down. You can still enjoy owning a business and work as the chief technician—like I love to do—but have all the freedom and fortune you want.

"Just keep focusing on the core five gears and *always* have a plan of action for improving yourself and each gear in your business.

"Today's guest is someone I met over five years ago in a very unusual manner. I had just finished meeting a client of mine for our monthly 'Geared for Growth' coaching session at his place of business. I love his waiting area and how he turned his industry standards upside down. So I tend to stick around after our sessions and enjoy his coffee and comfy couches.

"I happened to notice someone in the waiting room with stacks of paper and a tired, worn out, run down look on his face. Sound familiar? I know every business owner listening has faced this at some point.

"So anyway, I struck up a conversation with this gentleman and ended up taking him to lunch. I shared with him the five gears and he soaked it up like a sponge.

"He was ready to hear it and ready to live it.

"Now, his business has more than doubled, he takes over eight weeks' vacation a year, has a reliable team that handles the orders and management, and he runs the business as a true owner—not just an 'overpaid', or in many cases 'underpaid', worker. Folks, he is the real deal and he is here today to share some successes he experienced by using the core five gears to transform his business into a success and profits machine.

"Let me introduce you to Rick Baylor."

Chapter 32

HOW TO TRANSFORM

Bill and Rick exchanged pleasantries in conversation. They discussed their chance meeting and the way their conversation led to a detailed discussion of Bill's core teaching on the five gears and his 'Success and Profits Machine'.

Then Bill started into the real meat of the conversation. "So, Rick. I have two big questions for you that I think our listeners are dying to know.

"First, I want to know how in just five years you took your sign company from under a half a million dollars to now well over a million and a half in revenue with a great profit percentage.

"And second, I want to know what you would recommend our listeners do first to get the ball rolling, or that they add to their already implemented Machine plan."

Rick chuckled audibly over the phone and commented, "Bill, it sounds so good everytime you say that. Even when I say it... tripling my business in just over five years! A person just doesn't get tired of hearing or saying that!

"Let me first say that my life has been transformed as a result of this. I went from a business owner with a 60-hour a week plus 'job'—not a true business owner role—to now having more flexibility and freedom than I could have imagined. I have more time with my family, more time for fun, more fortune than I had in the previous five years, and time for putting my faith in action. And I still come in the office every now and then."

While the listeners obviously couldn't see Rick, it was evident he was smiling and happy as he talked. He continued, "Bill, whether divine providence or just chance that we met, that conversation changed me. I immediately went to work on my machine and the five gears. I sure am glad I took notes as we talked that day!

"I looked at each gear in my business and scored us on how we were doing. Conversation, Conversion, Captivation, Cultivation, and Cash Flow. I gave us a real grade on an A-F scale. Then I went through and came up with some measurable metrics for each one to give myself a benchmark.

"That was a scary and sobering process. We probably averaged about a D+, maybe a C- at best. I knew I had a lot of work to do. More importantly, I knew my customers wanted and deserved more. We were already pretty good at customer service and consistently had customers tell us we did a good job, but I knew we had more potential.

"In order to grow, we had to move each of our five gears from a C- to, at a minimum, an A. It was going to take work and even be painful at times, but I was committed.

"My first step was talking to my team. I shared my vision with them. They got excited and bought into the idea of being the best sign company in our region—even attracting clients in certain niches from all over the country. The kind of sign company that could choose who we wanted to work with and go get them.

"Once the team bought in, it was a matter of breaking down the overwhelming task of improving each gear into little baby steps.

"As an example, take Conversation. We knew we weren't doing a great job at this gear. We were okay at answering the phones, but not great. Certainly not using your 5-Star system. So we listed all the steps that would need to happen to help us improve. We did the same thing for our website, and for our other prospecting behaviors. We compiled the list and put them all up on a big board in a column labeled "Do" and then started moving them across the board to the "Doing" column and finally to the "Done" column until all had been completed.

"The best part was that we set a time frame for completion, and had weekly meetings to see who was working on what. The whole team was involved and everyone wanted to see it succeed. We consistently read our vision of being the best sign company in the region, being able to pick and choose the right customers and having revenues in excess of $1.3M.

"It worked great and we finished the first gear transformation in less than three weeks. Then we did the same for each gear until we had gone through all five.

"Once we completed all five, we went right back to the first gear and started over again. It is a continuous improvement plan.

"The next thing you know, Bill, we were doing $800k, then $1M... then we passed our goal of $1.3M and now we will be over $1.5M. The process worked incredibly well, and it keeps working for us today.

"Use this sytem and the process. Now about your second question... where would I recommend someone start?"

Chapter 33

THE FIRST STEPS

Bill interrupted Rick for just a moment to interject, "Rick, that's amazing, but I don't want my listeners to miss a very important point... you kept getting things done!

"That's a crucial distinction that every listener needs to understand, grasp, and make the mantra of anything they want to accomplish.

"Rick started doing things the very next day. He joined my coaching program and I only had to guide him a little along the process. His own motivation and drive kept things moving faster and faster.

"Okay, Rick, now tell our listeners where you would recommend starting today..."

Rick chuckled again and said, "Bill, you're so right. I remember getting home and telling my wife all the exciting things I had learned. She smiled, put her hand on my shoulder, and said, 'Relax, Rick. Take it one step at a time and keep on taking steps.' She was right, and I never stopped taking those steps.

"So where to start? Well, I strongly recommend doing just one thing. Go right now, well not right now—finish this podcast first—and call your business. Whatever your business is, call and pretend to be a customer. Ask dumb questions, yet buying questions, and see how your team handles it.

"This was the biggest revelation for me. I thought we were better than we were. We were certainly friendly, but we weren't closers. We weren't asking for sales, and we weren't capturing information and leads... two things you simply cannot afford to *not* do on the phones!

"Every business owner I now talk to and discuss the five gears with, I always tell them to go call their business right now and act like a customer. I have yet to have one come back to me and say they weren't surprised how bad it really was. Money was leaking out like you wouldn't believe!

"Fix the phones, then everything else will be built on that. I imagine this has something to do with why you placed that as the first gear. Right, Bill?"

"Guess I'm busted, Rick," Bill laughed. "But it probably also had something to do with $75k being lost every day at each of my business locations!"

They both laughed and Bill had a few closing comments and questions for Rick.

Rick wrapped up his interview by saying, "Anyone can transform their business. Even if you are already successful, if you take the five gears and work through them, you can find more opportunities for success. As you can tell, I'm passionate about it, and thanks to Bill I am now looking to tell as many people as possible to help them work on the gears in their own companies. In fact, I am starting a new business to help other sign companies grow their revenues and improve their life just as I did.

"Life's too short to be always working and rarely fully happy. Improve your business to make it what *you* want it to be... so you can live the life *you* want to live."

GETTING YOUR SUCCESS AND PROFITS MACHINE STARTED

This parable illustrates the possibilities that exist when you work through the five gears and put them into action to their full potential in your business.

As you saw from the story, any business can implement these five gears, consistently improve them and see massive results. You just have to be committed to systematically working on your business and not being held captive by your "job."

The work still has to get done, but if you have a system for working on the five gears regularly, you will see the growth results that you want to realize.

There are a few key steps to getting started on implementing your machine. Let's review each "Gear" and what you can do now to get started.

Remember to visit
GearedForGrowth.com/Bonus to gain
valuable resources to help you with each of the 5
Gears.

⚙ GEAR 1: CONVERSATION

Conversation happens anytime you engage with a new lead. It could be over the phone, on the website, through outside salespeople, advertising, or just meeting someone on the street. The conversation is always starting.

So what are you going to do to start the conversation out right?

Here are a few key steps to get you started:

1. **Fix your phones.** Have your business mystery shopped regularly. Train on how to answer, review it regularly, and reward.
2. **Review your website.** Is it absolutely clear what you want your potential lead to do when they get to your site? Don't have any confusion or too much information. Drive them to what YOU want them to do.
3. **List out all the ways you acquire new customers.** Review this list and identify which ones are the best producers. Make sure you know why they produce the best results and that they are repeatable processes.

If you start with these three Conversation Gear tune-ups, you will be off to a great start.

GEAR 2: CONVERSION

Conversion is all about creating a customer and increasing each transaction value. The goal is to convert as many prospects as possible at the highest possible transaction amount. For existing customers, it's all about increasing the amount of their next transaction.

What can you do to get started on increasing conversion?

1. **Increase your pricing.** Most business owners are very weak on this. You're losing margins if you aren't increasing prices on a regular basis.
2. **Have a firm follow-up system.** If you ever have any type of presentation, quote or proposal, or anyone who comes into your business, you must have a follow-up system. You can't convert what you don't follow up.
3. **Bundle services.** Don't just offer one thing, lump it together with other options. Whether a premium offering of the same service or product, or a completely different product or service which compliments it. Convert customers at a higher rate by packaging.
4. **Upsell.** Always have a next option. If you don't ask, you won't get it.

Start working on these four steps to increase Conversion and have a stronger transaction value.

GEAR 3: CAPTIVATION

Captivation is all about making such a great first impression that customers and clients not only talk about you, they come back again and again. The goal is to win them over as lifelong customers after their first experience with you.

What can you do now to start increasing your Captivation levels?

1. **Say 'Thank you!'** It's so rare to be thanked anymore. Not just verbally, but through a gift, note, letter, offer, or more.
2. **Follow up.** A simple call to see how everything worked out or to gauge satisfaction can go a long way. It's a powerful touch point.
3. **Make them another offer.** A buyer is a buyer. Making second offers as quickly as possible has a much higher rate of return than waiting or hoping they return. Get them back right away.

Start with these three simple steps and start Captivating your customers from Day 1.

⚙⚙ GEAR 4: CULTIVATION

Cultivation is all about growing and raising up better customers under conditions you can control. How can you make your customers better by doing things to bring them along? The goal is to get your lifetime average customer value higher and higher.

What can you do to create better lifelong customers?

1. **Create an engaging monthly PRINTED newsletter.** It may seem old-fashioned but it works.
2. **Make offers tied to events:** holidays, birthdays, anniversary dates, anything worth celebrating. Make an offer and have fun with your customers, but get them buying.
3. **Have a touch plan.** I recommend no less than thirty times per year for most customers. Mix it up by calling, emailing, mailing, or visiting in person. You have to be relevant and seen to get more business.

Customers love being loyal to good companies with great service and products. But don't wait on them to have a need. Drive the need and get the business.

⚙ GEAR 5: CASH FLOW

Cash Flow is all about having enough cash on hand to keep investing more in marketing than your competitors so your flow of leads and new customers never decreases, while theirs may wither and fade. The goal is to have consistent cash flow and profits to support continued marketing and sales efforts to create a sustainable, profitable business.

What can you do to get started?

1. **Set up an automatic savings plan.** Take a little money each week and set it aside. This creates your own internal line of credit and helps out when accounts receivable gets high.

2. **Have a regular system for accounts receivable follow-up.** You should always know the status of any accounts that get past 60 days.

3. **Invoice in a timely manner.** Don't wait to send out an invoice. Give customers and clients options to pay quickly. The more ways you have, the better your chance of getting paid quickly.

4. **Always know exactly how much cash you have in the bank.** This can be deceiving by relying on online banking—

because you are always taking in and sending out money. Know your balance!

Cash is still king. Many small businesses fail, not just because they didn't implement these five gears well, but because they thought just because sales increased cash would never run out. Manage your cash!

ONWARD TO SUCCESS

You now have the groundwork for a very successful business. Your Success and Profits Machine can start running as soon as you are ready to take action.

Implementing and monitoring the five gears is the core foundation of your future success. Don't let any excuse keep you from taking the next steps.

Congratulations on making it this far. You have already separated yourself from over 97% of other Americans just by finishing this book. Now become even more elite and take the next action steps.

There were several opportunities presented throughout this book to gain further resources to aid you in your Success and Profits Machine journey.

Visit: GearedForGrowthBook.com/Bonus

Thank you for committing to make yourself and your business better. You deserve the business you desire. Now go make it happen!

On to your Success and Profits Machine mastery!

Also available from this author:

Take Charge of Your Life:
Time Management Strategies to Help You Take Control of Your Time and Your Life

Tired of leaving the office feeling like you worked really hard, but unsure of what you really accomplished?

Do you wish you could get more done in a day and leave feeling like you really made progress?

Wondering how successful people really fly through projects and get things done?

This book covers basic strategies to help you take control of your time and get more done in the next month than you previously accomplished in the past year! Simple and effective strategies that can help you control your time and know you are making progress.

ABOUT THE AUTHOR

 Jon Toy is dedicated to helping others succeed. His goal is to help business owners double their business and work less! Through systematizing their business and increasing their customer touch points, Jon successfully helps business owners transform their businesses into Success & Profits Machines. Wherever you are in your business journey, Jon's helpful tips and strategies can help you grow your business and reach your goals.

He works independently as a business coach with many successful business owners and also offers large-group calls focused on using the '5 Gears' to grow your business and succeed, while achieving the right mindset to keep things moving.

He is a speaker and regularly motivates and inspires business owners to take action to transform their business. To contact Jon about speaking opportunities or coaching, email jon@jon-toy.com or visit www.Jon-Toy.com fo learn more.

Made in the USA
Middletown, DE
22 February 2016